Fires in Your Life

A Fire Expert's Guide To Preventing And Surviving Fires In Your Home

---

Lt. David A Wilson

An Ounce of Prevention is Worth a Pound of Suppression

"The first job of the fire service is the prevention of fire, not fire suppression. Only after fire prevention efforts have failed does the use of fire suppression techniques become necessary. Realize that when a fire breaks out, that is a failure of the system."

—Anthony Avillo

Deputy Chief (ret) North Hudson (NJ)

Regional Fire and Rescue

Contents

Introduction

I've been working in the field of Fire for my entire adult life. I was compelled to write an in-depth yet simple guide to helping everyone, no matter where they live or work, understand the dangers of fire and ways to survive a fire.

My book involves a lifetime of learning and applying those lessons to leave the world a better place than when I arrived on this planet, and had the pleasure of living in the greatest country in the world. A fire inspector is often the unsung hero of a larger fire organization. Fire prevention bureaus work day in and day out to prevent fires and, when they do occur, to lessen their impacts.

Most of us see the videos and pictures of fire scenes and the awards for rescues, and these are our first impressions of the modern fire service. Fire departments are groups that started under Ben Franklin, a great thinker and planner, who saw the need to protect people and buildings from the threat of fire.

My career in public safety was inspired in New Jersey by my dad's friend Joe Brunner, a navy veteran, EMT, and captain in the Hazlet First Aid Squad. Another role model was Al Riddle, my Sunday school teacher, and Nutley First Aid Squad member. I joined the Nutley Volunteer Emergency and Rescue Squad at the age of nineteen and met many great community members and my then-future wife, Dianne. I took every training course that was offered while moving up through the ranks and department chairs. Working with the American Red Cross gave me more opportunities to learn and experience tragedy in people's life. Some of my previous jobs included repairing small engines, preparing income tax returns, and direct selling of nutritional products. These experiences gave me the building blocks for the next stage of my career, and the vision to see that so many bad things are preventable.

The Nutley Fire Department was having an entrance exam, and this led to a job offering in 1985. The New Jersey Division of Fire Safety had been formed and a new Uniform Fire Code was to be implemented statewide. Help was needed and there was an offer of becoming a fire inspector and getting trained, along with a paycheck and benefits to support my wife Dianne and me. Taking the job became a golden opportunity to have a respected career and make a difference in my hometown.

The next twenty-five years were a whirlwind of training, inspections, investigations, fires, meetings, planning, natural disasters, interrupted dinners, late night calls, writing, and teaching. Dianne had to put up with a lot, and I thank her for the support and patience. Many local service awards were received and in 2007 I was promoted to Lieutenant.

This book will break down the many areas of responsibilities fire departments have, and be tied into many stories that reinforce the lessons learned for those who are looking to become a fire inspector.

Fires in Your Life will offer insight for those who just want to know more about what a fire prevention or fire protection specialist does. Firefighters and officers will get some insight into the planning and fire codes that make their job safer and easier. Property managers and homeowners will learn many vital fire safety lessons.

But most of all, I want you and your loved ones to keep this book as a life-saving guide, because you never know when fire may strike in your home, business, or elsewhere.

I hope you enjoy the read and get inspired to help make your little section of the world a safer, better place.

Lt. David A Wilson

1

Watching The Detective

Fire Investigations Ask:
Who, Where, When, Why, And How?

One of the more interesting and challenging duties a fire inspector has is determining the cause and origin of a fire. Many times the evidence is destroyed by the fire, stories change, people directly involved are injured or dead, fire suppression activities disturb the fire scene or there is a weather-related delay in the access. A fire scene can be a small area of a room, a dumpster, a whole house, or even an entire factory.

Safety for the investigator must take priority as there will be collapse hazards, weakened floors, smoldering debris, water both hot and freezing, electrical dangers, unknown chemicals or products, carbon monoxide, broken glass, protruding nails, bad weather, and hysterical occupants. You may be on location for many hours, long after the suppression crews have left the scene. You must plan for lighting, a partner, trash line or water extinguisher, personal supplies, food, water, and bathroom. You will need hand and eye protection, portable radio, cell phone, tools, camera, turnout gear, helmet, boots, high quality filter masks, or even a SCBA if working below grade.

I found the cell phone an important piece of equipment as I could now request other investigation services, equipment, utility crews, building officials, board up companies, and other support services without going through central dispatch. The dispatchers are all great people, but sometimes the fire jargon is misunderstood or requests get low priority attention if other emergencies are happening elsewhere. I recall one time we asked for a truck company on mutual aid and the dispatcher requested a fire truck, so the neighboring town interpreted the best they could and sent a pumper instead of a ladder truck, not exactly what we needed.

Remember now with all the millennials and other people as you yell out commands and requests, they don't know the "language" or terms you are using, so you will get what they think is best, not what you want. Be very specific and adjust to their level of knowledge and understanding. If you text it, you will probably get a better response.

Many fires are accidental in cause and are relatively easy to determine what happened, be it user error, stupidity, carelessness, or product failure. Results of an investigation in today's litigious society can have long lasting effect both positive and negative on families, businesses, insurances, manufacturers, individuals, and you. Put your ego on the shelf; if you can't make a determination, don't guess. There is no shame in not figuring them all out and a bad call on your end could open you and your agency up for lawsuits and public ridicule. Saying "it was electrical" is a common phrase that annoys me to no end. If electric caused as many fires as people say it does, we would have outlawed it years ago. The green agenda's conversion to all electric has added another twist as we see failures in lithium ion batteries and chargers increasing at an alarming rate.

The pressure will be great from family, media, neighbors, insurance adjusters, and public officials to know who, what, where, when, and why the fire happened. The process cannot be rushed, and if the fire is of a criminal nature, you could blow the whole case. Follow your agency's media policies and confer with the public information officer (PIO) assigned because once the words leave your mouth, you cannot take them back. There are many agencies that can help: local police, sheriff departments, prosecutor's office, state and county fire marshals, ATF, FBI, CPSC, and other large resources that you can tap for the really big investigations. They will have exposure to many types of fires and see trends that could help a larger investigation that is underway among their agencies.

There was a fire in a new home that was one week away from occupancy and the contractor was addressing the buyer's requests, which included staining and seal coating the wood floors. The weather was hot and humid and the central air conditioning and electric was turned off for economy. The work had been completed and the majority of the black plastic trash bags containing sawdust had been removed from the home. About 11:00pm that night, a passerby reported a house fire at that location. We arrived to find a fully involved one family house and worked for an hour or so to contain it and prevent fire spread to the other new house right next door. Extensive damage was done and the building was taken down to the foundation and rebuilt. The Arson Squad came in to help, due to high dollar loss and protocols we had in place for new construction. Five minutes after they arrived, it was determined a staple in a piece of Romex wiring was at the point of origin, so that was the cause. I made the case for the front hallway lobby floor being totally burned out and the builder saying he had left a debris bag there that day. There was no criminal act, so we closed our part of the investigation.

The next few months brought a flurry of OPRA requests and calls from the private fire investigators hired by six different insurance companies that had interests in claim settlements. A field meeting with all six private investigators was set, and I was excited to meet and observe some of the biggest East Coast investigators I had read about since my early arson training.

Well, the expected field debate did not materialize as all the teams held their opinions close to the vest. Realize that each was there to find a reason for the fire not related to their client. The biggest name investigator, a self-proclaimed god of cause and origin, took a small piece of wire, a staple and some charred wood into evidence for the lab. When I mentioned the trash bag with sawdust and the electric being off, he was rude and dismissive. Two of the other teams told me privately that I was probably right and not to be intimidated. The mediation that followed assigned losses to most of the contractor's insurance companies and the builder went on to rebuild and sell the house. The builder a few years later told me that he had become even more careful with floor sanding and always took the sawdust, rags, paper, and cans outside after doing the work and used metal cans for combustible debris.

Through the years, we have seen many floor refinishing fires, some by professionals and many by the do-it-yourselfers. The stain and the oil based sealers are combustible, so any rags, rollers, brushes, papers, and saw dust can spontaneously combust when conditions are right. The black plastic bags hold in the heat created, the sun coming in a window, the ember from a floor nail created during sanding, all can help complete the fire tetrahedron that has caused fires on loading docks, in a sawdust pile outside the home (up against the structure of course), in the hallways, in the garbage cans, and the back of a van.

We had one new business owner looking to get that rustic feel and save money doing it himself. That was my first experience with linseed oil being used on a floor and the rags left to combust, fortunately in a metal tray and below a fire detector, so damage was limited.

There was another similar circumstance where the contractor had set up a stain mixing lab on a front porch one summer day. The house was being renovated, and they were matching colors for the new window trim and moldings. The combustible vapors must have traveled into the ceiling of the porch and then into the attic where summer heat or the exhaust fan provided an ignition source. The owner was out walking his dog and returned to find the fire department cutting his roof and breaking windows, while fire hoses were being stretched into his front door and up the stairs. Another high value loss with many sports collectibles damaged and renovations back to square one.

We have seen people cleaning paint brushes with gasoline in the basement, next to the water heater or furnace. Houses improperly ventilated when refinishing floors and counters is another cause. Read the can and follow the warnings! A contractor using contact cement to put Formica countertops down without turning off the pilot lights on the stove and of course that was the last piece. Another fire induced "do over." Thankfully, new electronic ignition and sealed combustion chambers on hot water heaters and furnaces are all helping to reduce these events. Mechanics dropping gas tanks or dealing with bad fuel lines inside an enclosed garage attached to the house also lead to burns and bad fires.

The Home Center and Internet do-it-yourself lessons have created another source of fire causes. Many home repairs require a level of knowledge and tools that most homeowners do not have. Economic reasons, scheduling, finding a contractor, and spouse pressure all contribute to people working beyond their capacity. We have seen a person trying to change his stove without turning off the gas supply and without the benefit of non-sparking tools. Upon our arrival, we found the owner's brother-in-law holding the gas flex line out the door with the gas on fire, screaming for help. We turned off the gas valve in the basement and thankfully no one got burned, and the gas hose was long enough to reach outside.

We did see a plumber working on a branch shut off valve in an apartment building boiler room, without shutting off the main gas valve. The valve was old and crumbled under the wrench pressure and gas began filling the room. He had no putty to seal the line with and ignition soon occurred. Fire crews under fog line protection and with a very large wrench secured the gas feed before too much damage occurred.

Natural gas is safe until amateurs or cheapskates get involved, then watch out and call the utility company for help. You should have your gas shut off valves located and tagged so that during an emergency you or a responder can quickly shut down the gas supply. Having the correct wrench or disaster tool nearby is also a good idea.

Sometimes you will get several fires at the same address or involving the same family. Treat each one separately at first until some pattern emerges. You may find a juvenile fire setter, a drug lab, careless family, bad business plan without safety guidelines, elderly residents with diminished capacities, hobbyists, illegal home businesses, or a family member calling out for help. We had a young girl living with two uncles and several small fires occurred in their apartment. Upon investigation, we found the uncles had been abusing her, and these fires were a plea for help from her. We had the police and DYFS press charges and the girl was relocated to a safer environment. Don't miss those kinds of signals.

Another seemingly simple call with the doorbell chimes on fire within the living room turned into an escalating problem with that family. The twelve-year-old son was getting into serious fire play with encouragement from the father and lack of involvement from an alcoholic mother. We were starting to have many small fires at our ball fields, and he seemed to be in the area most of the time. Small trash fires became tire fires, then dugouts, and then bathrooms, storage trailers, and the like as his curiosity and skills grew. The Internet again was a source of inspiration and knowledge. We had him in for questioning and even a polygraph as investigations and fires continued. While watching one interview, it became apparent he was highly intelligent, savoring the experience and learning how to beat the polygraph. When he started talking in third person format during one interview, my hair stood on end as I realized this kid was big trouble and the lack of family support would be an impediment to our efforts.

He did sit through my Juvenile Fire Setter Intervention Course, but this was one time that I felt no connection with a student. The schools and police were concerned about escalation of his activities, but again family legal intervention kept him among the student body most of the time. There was quite a large fire at his home that almost killed his sister and father. He and a friend had made a matchstick cannon and fired it in the basement, setting many small fires that could not be stamped out and eventually involved the structure. We found his video camera among the debris and the entire incident had been documented. Thankfully, none of the fires injured anyone, and he went on to a drug problem and the family moved away. These juvenile fire setter problems can start out as very innocuous situations and then grow exponentially as their knowledge and juvenile justice system work in opposite directions.

Many juvenile fire setting issues can have underlying causes. I found many of the offenders had learning disabilities, such as ADHD, Asperger's syndrome, and other autism spectrum disorders, low IQs, or family issues. There would also be a tendency for these types to group together with none of them having good cause and effect skills to keep them out of trouble. Mental health workers will have to be involved to ensure proper treatment is obtained to correct these problems.

Some of the other mistakes people make are putting fireplace ashes in a cardboard box, then put- ting the box outside against the house, then going out for dinner. How about using a regular vacuum cleaner to clean up fireplace ashes? Putting the fireplace ashes in a plastic garbage can and then storing that in an attached garage. We have even seen ashes in paper bags! Now what school did they go to?? Ashes, especially from oak logs and other hardwoods can smolder for twenty-four hours or more and hot embers can survive even longer.

We have even seen the clean out shaft from the fireplace pit dump directly onto the basement floor and set a number of boxes on fire. This was the original design and the house had gone through several home inspections and sales over sixty years! You should never use the fireplace clean out door or pit for ashes unless it has been thoroughly checked out, and it directs ash to a safe place.

Charcoals from BBQ grills present a similar problem with disposal and safety. Lighter-fluid-soaked briquettes also have an elevated hazard if not stored properly. Never squirt lighter fluid onto lit charcoals. It can flash back to the can and cause severe burns. Long-handled tools, fireproof mitts, a garden hose, child safety zones, and cooking locations ten to twenty feet from the house are all part of safe grilling. I recall one gourmet-style super high-end cooking station that an owner put on his deck right up next to the home. That natural gas grill and hotplate had no real open flame, but plenty of heat. He melted about twenty rows of vinyl siding above the grill. There are these booklets called owner's manuals and installation guides that give you all the correct locations and use procedures. Very important instruction material that if followed, can prevent a tragedy. Never grill in a garage or fireplace with charcoal. The carbon monoxide will kill you.

While we are talking BBQs, let us touch on propane-fueled equipment. I have never liked propane tanks. Too many people have no clue how to handle these bombs. I see them stored in car trunks, basements, living rooms, attached garages, under decks, in the direct sunlight, on balconies to name just a few. New Jersey Fire Codes were changed many years ago to ban propane grills on balconies and within ten feet of multiple dwellings in response to many serious fires that occurred. One such balcony fire occurred in our neighboring town that destroyed two dwelling units and left the other twelve units uninhabitable for ten months while repairs were made.

The newer safety valves have helped a lot with limiting the leak points and ensuring better connections. The rubber hoses that connect the tanks are subject to UV degradation and critter damage. Apparently, those grease-soaked hoses taste quite good and many a hose fails during its lifetime. The cabinet enclosed tanks protect from these damages, but present a greater problem for suppression access when a fire occurs.

During one garage fire, a number of propane tanks failed and started coming down the driveway toward the firefighters. Bowling anyone? The specific gravity properties of propane keep the gases close to the ground and theses vapors can be very hard to disperse, and many times they will find an ignition source that will flash the whole vapor cloud.

No incident was more tragic than the father who was moving his family to Florida and wanted to take this BBQ and propane tank in the moving van. The movers said no full propane tanks on board, but he could empty it to make it safe. He went into the stockade fenced backyard and opened the valve to empty the tank. The vapors built up in the yard unable to disperse, until the bug zapper provided the spark to ignite the vapor cloud. Unfortunately, his daughter was in the yard and suffered second degree burns from the waist down. The burn center did a wonderful job saving her life and rehabbing her, but the scars will remain for a lifetime.

Another issue that was creating many runs for us occurred on hot days when the tanks would start to vent through their safety valves, releasing flammable gases into the yards and neighborhoods. We spent many a day behind trees and other protective covers using our fog streams to cool the tanks and disperse the gases. We finally found the local propane refilling station had a bad scale and poorly trained staff and was overfilling 20 lb. tanks all day long for weeks. The state police weights and measures team quickly fixed this issue.

Should you want to have a gas fired BBQ grill, I highly recommend you spend the money for a natural gas line with a remote shut off valve. Leaks will disperse quickly into the atmosphere, the odorant in natural gas is more detectable, and you will never run out of gas during a party. For all grills, read the manual and soap or leak test all hoses and fittings.

Storage of pool chemicals is another commonly misunderstood activity. Many chemicals are either water reactive or incompatible with other products and can be very corrosive. You must store these products out away from the home and pool in a cool, ventilated shed. Never store chlorine in the basement or garage, these products can kill you. Children should never be allowed to handle these chemicals and only adults with proper understanding of pool chemistry can do so safely. I recall a local pool club with a chlorine injector system in a pit. One day we arrived to see the owner scrambling and jumping into the pool. A supply line failed, and he had been sprayed with chlorine. The quick thinking jump into the pool saved him from burns on his skin and eye damage.

Dealing with injuries and fatalities at fire scenes is one of the worst parts of the job and is not for the faint of heart. The smell of burned flesh sticks in your nose and memory forever. Calculating the degree of burns and percentage rules gives you a sense of survivability for the victims. Knowing that the burn patient will undergo many months of rehabilitation and pain can reinforce your commitment to prevent fire and burn injuries. Most people that succumb to fire die from smoke inhalation and the associated toxic gases. The burned to death scenarios are less common but positively more gruesome. My early years in EMS exposed me to many horrible accidents, deaths, and injuries, so I thought I was ready for it all.

Most of us working in the emergency response field train heavily and this automatic response will kick in at the scene. Later, sometimes the same day or weeks after you can be affected by the memory in a bad way. Tears may flow for no apparent reason, a commercial or video may trigger a recall, nightmares or troubled sleep may occur, you may get very angry, you may stop socializing or doing the things you love, you may have suicidal thoughts, alcohol or drug abuse may occur. Our military calls it PTSD and you may need some professional help to get you over the event. Most agencies offer critical incident stress debriefing meetings, along with group and individual counseling that is run by wonderful people in the business that are highly trained in relieving your pain. The days of "I'm a tough guy no help needed here" are over. These effects can be cumulative as many bad events can occur throughout your career, so be aware of that in yourself, a coworker, or a loved one. This also makes the case for relatively short pension qualifications and career time. First, the physical part is obvious, the strength, stamina, and reflexes needed for the job are found in young people. Mental stress along with injuries and recuperative time only increase as you get older, this is a young person's job.

When dealing with injuries, the EMS takes over and transports the victim for further care and leaves you free for other duties. You may however need a statement from the victim, especially if they were alone. No one else will have the story. This can be hard but so critical to an investigation so you want to insert yourself into the patient assessment period before they leave the scene, if at all possible. A working relationship with the EMS and police should be established ahead of time and continually improved, so they understand your needs as an investigator. This may be the last time that victim is conscious or alive to make a statement.

One investigation involved a Sunday afternoon call for a house fire. We arrived to find fire in multiple locations in the home and a badly burned female on the front lawn. All the fires were small and even though there was no working smoke alarm the damages were limited. The quick interview in the ambulance helped us recreate the scene. Remember, I said these statements were important and in this case she was put into a medically induced coma at the burn center and died six months later without regaining consciousness. She stated that she had been smoking in the second floor bedroom, fell asleep, and then woke up on fire. The family was in the basement kitchen baking, and she had gone off to sneak a smoke at the second floor bedroom window, which is where we found an ashtray below the windowsill. The bed was adjacent to this, and we theorized that she fell asleep and the wind blew the ash tray contents onto the carpeted floor and bed. She awakened and realized her clothes were on fire and ran down the stairs and through the house trying to get help. The fire trail of burned clothes had ignited many small fires and her screams alerted the family in the basement. Smoking in the house, no smoke alarm, no stop, drop, and roll, poor ash tray placement, and no fire extinguisher all led to another preventable fire death.

Dealing with fire fatalities is a whole different level of documentation, compassion, and notifications. Many times a search and rescue operation results in removal of the victim for resuscitation efforts and transport to a hospital. These incidents need to be well documented for the investigation and possible recognition awards for the rescuers. Other fatalities may be obvious and left in place or discovered during fire overhaul procedures, either way, pictures, notes, sketches, and notifications must happen. The medical examiner, police detectives, coroner's office, state, county, and federal agencies may all be involved.

You are still the local authority in charge until such time you relinquish command. These agencies probably have much more experience and resources than you, so work along as a unified command to achieve a common goal. These agencies will have advanced methods for evidence collecting and testing. There may be specialists in church, factory, or chemical fires. The agency may have a canine unit that is trained in accelerant and explosives detection at arson fires. The body must be shown proper respect and consideration. Remember, this was a human being, someone's loved one or an innocent victim of a crime or accident.

When word starts to circulate that a fatality is on site, neighbors, busybodies, sightseers, insurance adjusters, media, and other unauthorized parties will try to get pictures, statements, IDs, and even try to access the scene. Call for help from the police to secure the perimeter, these intruders can cause major disruption of your scene, trampling or even removing evidence and valuables.

One particular fire resulted in the death of an elderly woman who was smoking and drinking in a lounge chair on the first floor. Her obvious demise led us to leave her in place for the coroner. Neighbors started congregating on the adjacent property to look in the windows to watch our well lit procedures. We realized the view needed to be blocked, so we raided the linen closet for sheets and blankets to block all the windows. Fire Dept. tarps and EMS sheets could also be used if needed. Remember, this is someone's loved one, not a wax museum or house of horrors display.

Another group to be controlled is your own firefighters. Once the fire is out and overhaul procedures are completed, the incident commander (IC) should be consulting with you on transferring scene authority. Some of the fire deaths can be quite gruesome with evisceration, exposed skeletal remains, dismemberment, or decapitation. You should preserve the scene and limit the firefighter's exposure to such tragic scenes for their mental health.

The onset of cameras being just about everywhere and the connection with social media can lead to instant unwanted widespread dissemination of pictures. Be sure your agency has a policy on this and absolutely everyone has to comply and enforce this mandate. Drones will become another privacy issue for us to deal with at fires and accidents.

Family pets are also a big responsibility we inherit after a fire. Pets that survive have to be accounted for and taken for medical checkups. A preplan for local animal hospitals, shelters, and SPCA should be in place. These pets will be agitated or injured and have to be handled by people with training. There are fire and EMS units carrying pet masks for their resuscitators now. Family pets that are killed should also be handled with dignity and compassion.

We had one dog die in a fire along with the owner, and I removed the dog's very ornate chain ID collar and placed it in a bedroom jewelry dish prior to the carcass being taken for disposal. The family a few weeks later asked what happened to the dog's remains as they wanted to have a service. We told them the dog had to be cremated after being unclaimed and the collar was in the bedroom dish. They were very thankful we had a caring attitude and preserved the collar to go over a picture of this little Boston pug that would sit alongside their late sister's picture.

Many times the family will be on scene during a fire and ask for things from the home before water and fire damage occurs. Picture albums, laptops, heirlooms, shoes, medications, cash, phones, and even cremation urns with ashes have all been on the request list. Retrieving these things and going above and beyond for the fire victims shows a fire department has a great caring attitude and results in good public relations.

There are many ways to get trained in fire investigations, including on the job (least desirable), college courses, fire academies, and criminal justice departments. Whatever path you take, apply yourself at every level because someday you may be subpoenaed for a deposition or court testimony and the lawyers will attempt to qualify or disqualify you as an expert witness. Class A dress uniforms or fancy suits will not qualify you for anything other than well dressed.

Photographic documentation will be critical for your case. I cut my teeth using 35 MM SLR film cameras and this was great for many years, although hard on our budget and storage. When digital cameras came out, it was better than sliced bread. We could take dozens of pictures, the cost was low, and storage space was easy using removable discs. Copying and printing became easy and the bosses appreciated the reduced cost. You may be fortunate and have an assigned photographer or you may be doing it all. Either way, try to get those early in the fire external shots immediately, as the building may be gone or in a pile when the day is over. Origin areas for a fire help to limit your digging in the ashes and can support or dispel statements from occupants or workers.

There were many times I took different angles of a shot in a room and found the camera and flash highlighted or supported something that was not obvious to the naked eye. Sometimes the owners will try to pad their insurance claims or blame the firefighters for "missing" jewelry. A few camera shots of the supposed area of loss and soot patterns can make the story change quickly. Many times a fire can be a burglary cover-up, so things may be missing from the scene. Be sure the police help you on these cases.

Storage of pictures and reports should be in a locked area and properly logged so the chain of custody file is intact. Retention of these files should follow the legal guidelines established by your prosecutor's and attorney general's office. Try to always work in teams or pairs so you have a witness to your activities in case someone makes an accusation against you or your partner.

Investigation of fires can be rewarding, frustrating, life-changing, and inspirational all rolled into one. Use your talents, knowledge, and training to not only solve the case, but put the bad guys in jail. Develop juvenile fire setter intervention programs, initiate a product recall, author a press release, or start a fire education program based on your findings. Lobby for fire code changes, document fire sprinkler and smoke alarm performance, and influence fire suppression SOPs. Helping to make society more fire safe are all benefits of a good cause and origin investigation.

2

===

Clothes Dryer Fires

How To Dry Your Clothes Safely

We have come a long way from taking our clothes down to the river, beating them with a stick, and then hanging them from the nearest tree to dry. Inventors designed machines that could actually get clothes clean in the privacy of our home and then we would hang them outside on clotheslines for drying and public display. Weather, birds, pollution, and manufacturers pushed inventors to make that magic machine that could dry, de-wrinkle, and make our clothes smell fresh, all without lines and clothespins. There were many designs, accessories, and gadgets that made the job quicker, cheaper, and in many cases exposed you to a greater risk of fire.

Improper venting, poor installation, and lack of maintenance continue to keep clothes dryer fires in the top ten causes of residential fires year after year. I have been on a thirty-year crusade to educate home-owners about the many ways this labor-saving appliance can cause a major fire in your home and how you can make things safer.

The National Fire Protection Association (NFPA) reports that there is an average each year of 15,970 home structure fires involving a clothes dryer or washing machine. The vast majority of these fires (92%) involved clothes dryers

First, let us look at locations for these dryers. Somewhere in the basement, first floor laundry closet, and second floor laundry room are all places that should a malfunction occur, the structure, voids, or building systems will be directly impacted by the fire. We load up the machine and go on our way, whether to do other chores, talk on the phone, play on the computer, or worst of all, leave the home. When a problem happens, it is very unlikely anyone will be nearby to detect the fire or take action until it is too late and fire department response is needed.

We had a call for a basement fire one evening and arrived to find lots of smoke and flames showing. The neighbor who discovered the fire saw the owners leave earlier and no cars were present. We forced entry into the home and did a primary search and then started our fire attack after calling a second alarm. The fire had started by the basement clothes dryer and got into the walls and traveled to the attic. Major structural damage occurred and all the electric and PVC plumbing systems had to be replaced. Smoke damage throughout the home was extensive and reconstruction took almost a year.

Sometimes, it is just a matter of not piling the clothes up against the dryer, so that if something occurs, you won't have fuel for the fire. Knowing how your machine works is important, so read the manual that comes with it and take note if the clothes are taking longer to dry. This is the first sign of clogged or improper venting.

All dryers, either gas fired or electric, must be vented to the exterior of the building according to manufacturer's instructions. Gas dryers make carbon monoxide (CO), a deadly byproduct of combustion. All dryers, with the exception of some high-end ventless models, make some kind of lint and steam. This is a health and fire hazard and a cleanliness issue. The dryer ducting should be hard pipe, not flexible plastic hoses or cheap foil hoses that are designed for bathroom vent fans. The "knock test" is one way to ensure that the vent is of proper material.

The vent run should be less than twenty feet long and direct as possible. Some newer dryers can vent up to thirty-five feet, so check your instruction manual for details. Do not use long screws to hold the pipe together. Instead use very short screws, pop rivets, band clamps, or special duct tape designed for that use. You want the interior of the pipe as smooth as possible so no lint gets caught and cleaning is easy.

There are some special inline boost fans that can be used when an excessive length of vent is used. The termination flapper should be a full open, hooded flapper, or gravity energy saver ball. Do not use the flat three-flapper type or critter guard. These will all catch lint and lead to a clog. I was inspecting a new house renovation and the owner said her new dryer was junk and wouldn't dry the clothes. We looked to see how the second floor laundry was vented and on the outside was a critter guard totally clogged with lint. We got a ladder and removed that critter guard, problem solved.

I have seen dryer after dryer that wouldn't dry the clothes, vent runs forty feet long, lint plugs in the line that would fill a bucket. Also under deck runs that are so cold the steam can't make it out, venting into chimney with furnace and hot water heater, termination points into crawl spaces under the home. I have observed dryers just vented into the room or basement and connected to a useless water trap. Trying to use old stockings to "catch" the lint and carbon monoxide doesn't work. It is dangerous to have inline vent diverters so the heat from the dryer can be used to warm the basement. Crazy and unsafe installations, all true.

We performed a home safety inspection for a family that was going to have triplets soon and wanted some advice on alarms and egress. We also found that she was planning to use cloth diapers and would be doing her own laundry. Yikes! Despite the husband's best efforts, the lint accumulated and a small fire occurred.

Duct work should be cleaned out at least once a year and can be done by professionals. Seek out local service technicians who are trained and equipped to handle your venting needs. If you are handy, good brushes, lint lizards, shop vacuums, tools, electric blowers, and mechanical background will all be needed.

When installing concealed duct work or vertical runs of pipe, a clean out port should be engineered into the system to help with this maintenance. Cleaning is another reason to not use flexible ductwork; it will tear easily and have to be replaced.

Another area of thought is the dryer fabric softener sheets. These can leave an invisible film on the lint screens inside the dryer, which can restrict exhausting and potentially lead to a fire inside the drum. A simple water test performed under the faucet will show if the water can't pass through the lint screen, neither can the steam and heat. Take an old toothbrush or soft nail brush and carefully clean this screen every six months. Replace lint screen insert if damaged.

Machines that get a lot of use or are over twenty years old should be watched closely for malfunctions. Damaged clothing, long drying periods, different sounds during operation can all be signs of trouble brewing. Have the machine checked by a professional and replace if needed. Follow instructions for items that are dryer safe and be sure to adjust the heat settings as noted on the care tags. New machines should be energy star rated and sized for the household loads.

The flexible gas line should be replaced with a new installation. The old brass colored flex lines were recalled back in the mid-eighties due to solder joints cracking. New flex lines should be stainless steel and have a yellow coating along with a testing agency approval label. Professionals should be doing these installations.

Lastly, the product registration card should be filled out and sent in. This should help in the event of a safety recall, so you will be notified. The Consumer Product Safety Commission website also tracks recalls and is a great way to check all your appliances and toys.

There was the case of a homeowner buying the best high-end dryer made and had a real quality installation done. She loaded the dryer and went upstairs to bake cookies. Her husband gets a text from the alarm company that the smoke alarm is activated. He calls her and she thinks it must be the cookies in the oven, but he says no, it is the basement alarm. That new model dryer had a history of malfunctions and was the subject of several large fires and a safety recall. The firefighters arrived, mitigated the situation, and consumed the cookies.

Having a working smoke detector in the vicinity of the dryer is a very prudent move. I have a personal preference for electric dryers. No gas line to leak, no CO issues, energy efficient models, less fire danger, and cheaper to purchase. Make dryer checks a regular part of every home inspection for both yourself and the public. Make it a family policy to never leave the home while appliances are operating or you may not have a home to return

3

Animals At Homes And Businesses

Saving Your Pets From Fires

There's no doubt that millions of Americans are living a love story with their pet. As of 2024, pets live in 86.9 million American homes! 65 million homes have a dog; 46.5 million cats live with pet owners and 11.1 million fish swim around in tanks found in US households.

It makes sense that you make a plan to keep your pets safe in case of a fire in your home. But you must always remember: no matter how much you love your pet, it is critical you leave the premises if necessary to survive.

Many critter habitat fires occur when ground prongs are removed from electrical plugs, heat lamps are too close to combustible items, pumps overheat, extension cords are overused, adults do not supervise the children's space or makeshift repairs are done to electrical items. The fire you prevent could save the pet and the family.

Animals can be responsible for fires in other ways. They may chew on electrical cords, knock over lamps and candles, activate switches, urinate on electrical outlets, and even fly around with their tails on fire from a halogen lamp or flame.

One particular fire involved a large residential loss under suspicious circumstances. The owner was sure that his cat had stepped on the switch for the toaster oven, upon which he had left his newspaper. The ensuing fire that occurred while he went on a job interview consumed the kitchen, artwork, collectibles, and contents, all on his inventory list, and even killed the St. Bernard dog. The cat would admit to nothing and the owner was given a polygraph twice with inconclusive results, so the insurance company eventually had to settle the claim.

A final thought on birds in the homes. Most birds are caged, just keep your fingers out and all will be fine. Some owners will allow free flight within their home, and they should make you aware of this so you do not open exterior doors until bird is isolated or they may escape. Some birds will land on your shoulder, again be aware, so your swatting instinct doesn't endanger the bird. A lot of the larger birds, such as African Grays, Macaws, parrots, and other tropical birds are quite valuable and can outlive their owners; respect the family-like attachment. These birds can be trained for tricks and talking, enjoy the show if you have time. One bird even mimicked the smoke alarm, probably not the best trick he learned.

There is a very interesting connection between hoarders and cats. Many hoarders keep multiple cats around, just another part of their "collections." Many towns have attempted to limit the number of cats in apartments and homes, but were met with very organized and well-funded opposition groups that derail these well-intentioned laws that would control disease, eliminate filth, prevent building damage, control stench, protect songbird populations, and control feral cat colonies.

One particular house fire brought us to a home that was occupied by a cat rescue person, who actually was approved by several towns for cat removals. The problem became evident when we entered the home that all the cats had been relocated to her home and were breeding everywhere. The entire home was a litter box and the felines were in poor health, malnourished, dead, and diseased and now had smoke inhalation issues. The total count of live and dead exceeded one hundred cats, and we spent a good part of the day trying to account for all the cats, catch them, and then get treatment. The occupant, who appeared quite normal and well groomed, had even named all the cats. The scene was out of a horror movie, with cats in every cabinet, in the walls, in the freezer, buried in the yard, all with a stench that was unbelievable. Many cat rescue groups started showing up in private cars and taking cats to vets throughout the area. Media coverage was of course extensive, and we set up tents and tarps as a staging area to control the scene.

Many fire departments and EMS groups now carry resuscitation masks that are made for dogs and cats. These are used to revive a pet suffering from smoke inhalation. Animal rescue groups will donate these to any organization seeking to equip their vehicles with these masks. This is a win-win public relations move for everyone.

Fire Inspectors and Pets

One of the many experiences a fire inspector will have is dealing with animals: the four-legged kind. There will be many types of pets you will encounter on your travels including snakes, hamsters, gerbils, lizards, iguanas, fish, birds, and the occasional exotic animals. Observe the critters and engage the owners for some entertainment that will break up your day a little.

Many people keep pets that range from dogs to cats, birds, snakes, and pretty much anything that can be domesticated or caged. This visit can be a fun side benefit as you inspect people's property or it can be a nasty surprise when that pet attacks. Most people are responsible owners and will have either a warning sign posted or will greet you at the door and explain their pet's behavior or the steps they have taken to secure the animal. Having background as a dog sitter in my younger years, reading articles and watching videos from dog trainers has given me good insight into animal behaviors, and I have been bite and attack free for my entire career. The old saying "every dog has its bite" cannot be ignored and you must always remember that you are a visitor to their territory. Many dogs have a protective instinct of the property, family members, and their food, so you must be aware of your positioning in relationship to the dog, especially if multiple family members are present. Dogs are pack animals and will protect the pack.

Let's focus on dogs for a minute, as these are the pets most likely to challenge you when visiting homes or businesses. The family dog can be the tiny yipping ones that give you a headache making it hard to talk with the owner. The medium, fast dogs that run down the steps with you as you try not to trip or step on them. They can be that lovable golden retriever, sheepdog or black Labrador that gives you a pants leg full of hair or slimes you. You can also be exposed to Rottweilers, pit bulls, Dobermans, shepherds, and other dogs that can be aggressive when treated badly, especially when trained as attack or fighting dogs. Many dogs are rescue, strays, or other unknown backgrounds taken from the animal shelters, so there can always be some trigger for a bad memory in that dog's life. My neighbor had a female Rottweiler that strayed into his flower shop one day, so he brought her home.

The dog was pleasant, affectionate, and would lean on my feet and legs when I visited. Then one day I was walking up the driveway, and she started growling with her hair rising up, classic signs of aggression. I backed away as the owner secured her, and we talked about it and found her nephew had similar issues all the time. The common thread was we both had baseball caps on. He wore his all the time, and I wore it just this one time when she growled. Someone in the dog's previous life must have been abusive who wore a cap.

Uniforms can be another trigger for dogs acting out. We all know the mail carriers are rarely accepted by dogs, maybe it's the bills and junk mail. More importantly, whenever they bark, the carrier continues on his way, so the dog becomes confident that he can chase away anyone in uniform with a few well-timed barks, snarls, and growls. Every dog is different, some bark a lot, some are really quiet, big, small, curious, protective or just loveable.

Whenever you approach a building look for the dog indicator signs: leashes, water bowls, brown spots in lawn, poop, scratched or bitten door frames, slobbered glass, moving window blinds or shades are all signs that a dog lives here.

When approaching a fenced-in yard, I always shake the gate and whistle, lest I get in the yard and come face-to-face with a dog who has never met me. This also brings me to another point. Never run from a dog as they will chase you every time, to bite or play with you, but you won't know which one until it is too late. Back away from a dog and talk calmly, try some voice command: sit, stay, lay down, or other such actions. Try and get something to protect you if an attack is expected, big stick, garbage pail, clip board, lawn chair, or other item. Perhaps throw a ball in the other direction or create a remote distraction.

Should there be multiple dogs, a few prayers would probably help if the pack mentality is taking hold and the owners are not around or can't get control. I always carry a few dog biscuits in my pocket. These can be used to make friends, just get owner approval in case the dog is on a special diet. Treats can be used as a distraction with some dogs, but realize that a true guard dog is probably trained not to accept food from strangers.

The dogs will take cues from their owner's response to your visit. Most visits are routine, checking new furnaces, fireplaces, dryers, and smoke alarms, but occasionally your visits can be confrontational and dogs will sense this and will take their master's side. Watch for barring of teeth, rising of their back hair, lowered head position, lowered non-wagging tail, growling, frenzied barking, and a general change in demeanor.

You will run into anti-government people, known as sovereign citizens, who may use their dogs to intimidate or even attack you, so watch for those occupancies and avail yourself of police assistance. Criminals selling drugs and supplying dogs for fighting rings can also harbor vicious animals, and you must have police and dog handlers present at these locations.

Whenever you enter a building with a dog, always talk cheerfully with the owner and then make friends with the dog. Extend your non-dominant hand in a closed fist, under the dog's nose and let him smell you. This is less threatening than over his head and puts him at ease to investigate you. If he does decide to bite you, then your fingers are not extended to be damaged or locked onto and most dogs can't handle a whole fist in their mouth. Scratching under their jawline and on their throat is generally a good way to cement your bond and gain permission to enter into their domain.

I always stay away from babies and dog food dishes because protective dogs may take action to "redirect" you. Dogs in cages or crates can be talked to, but never attempt to pet them or stick your hand between the bars.

Another practice to help endear you to the owner and dog is to ask prior to testing the fire alarms, that they put the dog and baby outside away from the noise. The decibel level from multi head systems and low voltage systems can easily exceed 100 dBs and the pitch can really hurt a dog's and infant's ears. The dog could get frenzied and nip at you, start howling, or at the very least negatively associate you with future visits.

Some other things to think about are dogs that are cooped up all day or don't get a lot of visitors can get excited and lose bladder control or defecate on the floor, so watch your step. I have dodged many "land mines" in the house and outside. One particular case we discovered after a house fire revealed the basement floor was the dog run for many years and was quite disgusting, requiring boots to enter and decontamination as we left the scene.

Most family dogs are vaccinated against rabies. Should you get a wound of any type from the animal, the owner should provide documentation of shots so you can plan your course of treatment, which can range from simple wound cleansing to a series of painful abdominal rabies shots.

Dogs can rub up against poison ivy and carry the oils on their fur, so after contact with dogs you should wash with very hot soapy water to prevent any itch problems. Fleas and ticks can also be carried by the dog, so personal tick checks and even insect repellant sprays may be indicated at certain occupancies.

Any dog foaming at the mouth, showing distemper signs, barring his teeth, displaying hackles, or causing your neck hairs to stand up should be avoided completely. No inspection is worth getting injured over, tomorrow is another day.

There are many things to think about when performing inspections, not just the technical side of what you do. Dogs can be a lot of fun, I even "deputize" the really friendly, inquisitive dogs who follow me all around the house, so don't be afraid to make a new friend.

Cats can be another common house pet and they range from friendly to scared to downright nasty. Most felines run and hide when you enter the home, and you never have to deal with them, just watch out for litter boxes, toys, and spilled food. I never bother to make friends with the cats because they just don't care and the hair and spittle can aggravate any allergies you may have.

We came across one particularly aggressive cat, when a superintendent and I were inspecting an apartment. The cat, a big orange tabby, was on the kitchen table eying us up when he jumped onto the superintendent's leg and starting clawing him through his jeans. He kicked the cat off, but it came back to attack again. After being pushed off again, the cat turned his attention toward me. I had to use my smoke detector test stick and clipboard to fend off his attack, just like a lion tamer at the circus. There may have been some prior history between that cat and super that instigated this attack.

The Cat in the Tree and Other True Stories

No fire service book would be complete without a cat rescue story. A kitten had been stuck in a tree for about a week and the neighbors had tried everything to coax the cat down, including lots of cat food. The cat would cry at night interrupting everyone's sleep and the local children were quite upset. Many agencies had been contacted, but no help was forthcoming. The standard response was "Have you ever seen a cat skeleton in a tree?"

Many fire departments have shied away from cat rescues due to OSHA regulations and the injuries sustained by firefighters trying to do a good deed. Our public safety commissioner got wind of the trapped kitten and ordered the captain to take his crew and "get the damn cat out of the tree." They arrived to find the kitten about forty feet up a large, vine-covered oak tree in the backyard, inaccessible to the ladder truck or any ground ladders.

The kitten truly appeared to be unable to climb down and a large crowd of spectators began to gather. The engine had a high pressure water pump, and it was decided to wet the cat with the booster line and encourage it to come down. Well of course you know what happened next. The cat got spooked, lost its grip, and took a long drop with legs spread, bounced off a garage roof, rolled to the ground, stood up, and ran away without so much as a thank you. The kids cheered the firefighters and provided lemonade for all. This was before the days of wide-spread video devices. There is no record other than our memories, but what great memories they are!

One summer a girl took her parrot to the park to show him the great outdoors. She had his perch and the wings had been clipped so he shouldn't have been able to fly. Well those feathers grew back and off he went into the trees, resulting in a call to 9-1-1. The truck company laddered a few trees and the bird flew away each time we got close, quite a comedy show. Finally, with a pike pole, we pulled a dead limb he had perched on and tackled him as he rode that branch all the way down. Most recoveries do not go so well, the temperatures and predators usually make for a sad ending.

A neighbor of mine has birds and has taught me a lot about recovery. Many are perched trained so they may come down to your finger or stick, have a treat ready. Many owners train the birds to the Andy Griffith Show whistle melody as a way to bring them in if they escape. Watch for nips on your fingers and have their cage ready for them to enter.

Wild animals are another issue that presents challenges. Turkeys, geese, bears, deer, raccoons, snakes, skunks, and other critters can create havoc in a neighborhood where you may find yourself inspecting. Habitat destruction has forced many animals into residential areas and unschooled residents feed these "cute" critters, imprinting them, making the problems even worse as the animals lose their fear of humans.

Educate yourself on animals in your area and if needed, invest in repellent sprays or devices. Most wild animals want to avoid human contact and will go the other way. The exceptions are when babies are nearby, you corner them, they are ill or you threaten them in some way.

An aggressive male turkey in the neighborhood loved to attack the mail carriers, so much so that mail delivery was stopped until the tom was captured and relocated. I guess the turkeys hate junk mail too, but I suspect the red, white, and blue of their logo was a challenge to his territory.

Canada geese can be aggressive if you approach their chicks or nest, and they are poop machines so watch where you step. Raccoons and birds can nest or get stuck in chimneys so be careful when you open the fireplace damper for an inspection. Farm visits should always be with the farmer or staff member, especially if they have a bull on the property.

Honey bee apiaries may also be present in the yard. They are usually stacked boxes with a small opening at the bottom. Honey bee colonies are usually very passive, and they just go about their work collecting pollen. The best advice is stay out of their flight path or "bee highway" in front of the hive. Kicking or opening the hive would be ill advised also, as the bees would view this as an attack and come out to protect the queen. The beekeeper will suit up and smoke the hive to calm the bees before opening the apiary to collect the stored honey. Most stings you get are from yellow jackets, wasps, or other aggressive insects that you annoyed by getting too close to a ground nest or you swatted at them. Water from a hose or jumping into a pool is the best way to get the attack scent off your body if you find yourself under assault by the bees.

I have a honey bee apiary in my yard for several years and only got stung once when I knelt on a poor honey bee that was just trying to get away. These bee colonies are fascinating to learn about and watch as they go about their daily chores. My organic garden is way more productive due to the increased pollination action, and we get some great honey from the colony.

Finally, as you go about your fire duties, other things may come to your attention that appear or you know are wrong. Animals can be mistreated, abused, left in hot cars, etc. Refer any suspicions you may have to appropriate agency, be it police, animal welfare group, SPCA, or mental health agency.

If you see something, say something. Fire inspectors are one cog in the wheel rolling through every town and city making quality of life issues everyone's job.

4

Hoarders

Your Clutter Can Kill You

We have all seen the pictures, newspaper articles, and TV shows with extreme hoarders. The Collyer brother's mansion, famous people, your neighbor, friend, or maybe someone in your own family can all suffer from this addiction, obsession, disorder, or whatever tag you want to attach, but it is real and can adversely affect a person, family, neighborhood, or even a whole apartment complex. Obsessive compulsive disorder (OCD) is often cited as an underlying cause, but it can be a traumatic event, medical condition, depression, family lifestyle, or other impact, so be ready for a long-term, sustained effort to correct these situations.

I have noticed that people who lived in the 1930s and 1940s during The Great Depression and WWII, which caused many people to be without basic necessities and money, will still have that need to save for the next rainy day. This need, along with diminishing mental and physical states, can lead to a nightmare of saved garbage, multiple dish sets, old broken furniture, newspapers, toys, or clothes. "I might need it someday" or "It will come back in style" or "I have someone who wants it" or "I can get money for it" or "I need a spare" will be among the many excuses you hear. The disorder is not limited by age however as I have worked with many hoarders of all maturities that you will get to meet in the stories that follow.

The past several decades have been an amazing time for inventions, increased wealth, and improved living standards. With this comes the ever increasing obsolescence of just about everything we own, so we strive to keep up with society, but create mountains of debris in this quest. When the old stuff accumulates in the building and yard then safety and health issues start to develop. This is when the fire inspector, code enforcement officer, and housing inspector get involved.

Some hoarders "display" their stuff in the yard and garages, so these locations can be easily spotted. The hoarders that keep it all inside their home or apartment will be the ones that go undetected until some event brings emergency responders or health workers to the home. Be ready for overwhelming smells, bugs and insects, contamination, rotted food and garbage, dangerous conditions, electrocution hazards, poor lighting, blocked exits, no heat, bedridden residents, booby traps, and mental states of all types.

Hoarders acquire their goods many ways including inherited, bought on sale, trash and curb picked, shoplifted, freebies, garage sales, borrowed, donated, and other ways. The main thing is more goes into the home than comes out so it fills up room by room until living conditions become untenable. I set a policy in our home known as the "One in Two Out Rule," so we will keep the home reasonably clear of excess accumulations.

The small collections, along with family heirlooms and mementos are not the target of the average cleanout effort. The newspapers from thirty years ago, outdated clothes, old financial records, broken electronics, old photos with no names or dates, cracked dishes, old shoes, boxes in the attic unopened in twenty years, these are some of the easy cleanouts we can do ourselves. Then there are the big projects that require really good friends, professional help, dumpsters, and maybe even heavy equipment.

Apartment buildings and other multiple-dwelling-type structures are very important target hazards that must have hoarders identified and corrected. When an occupant creates a hazard that can affect not only themselves, but other tenants, neighbors, emergency responders, inspectors, repairmen, maintenance staff, and owners, action must be taken. Hoarders cause odors, insect and rodent infestations, egress issues, lack of cleanliness, structural collapse, and fires.

Think about that filled up unit and how an EMS crew would be challenged to give care and remove a victim. Think about how the inspector could not access the rooms to check electric, egress windows, and smoke alarms. Think about how the occupant would escape a fire or other emergency. How would fire personnel be able to perform a search and rescue operation? Think about maintenance staff trying to repair electric or plumbing issues.

When doing routine inspections, look out for the units you did not access. They may be hiding a hoarder. Well-run complexes usually make annual checks in the units and will address the issues before they become severe, but sometimes they will be looking for your help. Housing codes will address the responsibilities of the owners and tenants, so the legal remedy will be your trump card if needed.

The first attempt will be to visit and document the situation, including interviewing the occupant and getting family details. Should there be any children living in such a unit, then local police and child welfare agencies will need to be involved. You should also have a team of healthcare workers, legal aid, mental health agency, senior advocates, and other inspection agencies that may have jurisdiction. These will be difficult cases needing a lot of brain power, stamina, patience, and experience.

Having a team may also provide you with a person the occupant can bond with, and they can play "good cop" versus your "bad cop" role. There must be a written violation issued per your agency's protocols as the first step toward remediation. The mental and physical help part comes later as you identify the needs of the occupant. Remember, you are helping not just the occupant, but also neighbors and family that can be affected by this condition, so enlist their assistance when possible.

One unit we found during routine inspections consisted of a middle-aged female who kept every article of clothing and footwear from her entire life. There were racks, storage boxes, shoe trees, hats, coats, and chest of drawers in every area of this two-bedroom apartment. Many of the articles were brand-new, not her size, and never worn so this tipped us off that she was a hoarder. The unit had not been cleaned in quite some time and the dust layers and cobwebs were incredible. We spoke with her and were met with some hostility, which is common. On this visit we got her daughter's contact information and developed a plan. Our written violation turned out to be important as the clean out efforts failed to progress. Next, we went to municipal court. The judge was supportive of our actions and read her the riot act and gave some deadlines to meet or else. This brought family members and professional help in to rectify the situation within two months. This was one of our easier projects.

Another unit was one of the more bizarre apartments we did not get access to during our routine visits. The landlord was concerned that many items were being carried into the unit and her car was packed full of stuff. We met this thirty-year-old, former army member and now secretary who seemed quite pleasant and well groomed. The apartment was filled beyond capacity with craft projects, garbage, clothing, and just plain junk. There were no walkways. We had to walk on one to two feet of debris. The bathroom could not be entered. There was no access to the bed. The kitchen cabinets could not be closed due to all the contents spilling out. The refrigerator was filled with old food and drinks. The oven was packed with stuff. The closets were jammed, and she shared this unit with two free range ferrets.

We did a lot of mental health actions with her including counseling but were not making much headway. I still wonder to this day where she slept, ate, and did her daily hygiene. During one visit, we could only get her to fill one small bag with stuff she did not need. All the rest was for craft projects and mementos she said. She was not argumentative or combative, so I guess our compassionate side overwhelmed our enforcement side and the case dragged on for over a year.

This case came to a dramatic ending when a fire was reported in her apartment. She had a lit candle on the windowsill that ignited a windblown curtain. She attempted to use a fire extinguisher first. Then she retreated to pull the fire alarm. This action alerted everyone to escape and sent a signal to the dispatch center. Fire was blowing out her window upon arrival of the first alarm assignment. Fortunately, the fire was contained to her unit, with some water damage in the two units below. The fire overhaul process gave us the opportunity to empty the contents out into the parking lot, enough to fill two dumpsters. Sadly, the ferrets succumbed to the fire and she picked through the pile trying to salvage whatever she could. Her lease was not renewed, and we lost track of her. Hopefully, she received medical help and is living a more normal life.

Another case we had in an apartment that started with a tip from the superintendent who wanted to do work in this unit occupied by a forty-five-year-old female. This was a small one-bedroom apartment overloaded with clothes, books, cooking supplies, furniture, music collection, a bicycle, and storage containers. We interviewed her and made some suggestions on putting some things into storage or getting a larger apartment. The super had a contentious relationship with her, and we found out she was a paralegal. This would be a challenging case. She rearranged things to make more space but did not remove items to storage. Her defense was financial hardship and the need to be with her possessions. I would see her briskly walking to the bus in her black legal outfit and was reminded of Elmira Gulch from the Wizard of Oz. We parried back and forth over the years and one time I received a three-page letter stating her positions and providing measurements in the hallway, bedroom and kitchen down to one-half inch that proved her compliance with the housing code. One of my administrative assistants knew her from high school and recalls her being difficult and a loner.

Single family homes with hoarders can be the hardest to identify and correct. A person's home is their castle mind-set and legal precedents can really slow down the process of intervention. Usually, a medical call or social worker referral starts the case. Sometimes a contractor doing work or taking out building permits can also be the source of identification. I have noticed that the engineering and inventor types have a tendency to save a lot of junk for their next project. One local home has sixty years' worth of parts and discarded projects piled up in the basement. The owner claims affiliation with nuclear, space, and government agencies. He stated all these items are needed for research purposes.

A welfare check brought us to a home inhabited by a seventy-year-old recluse. The house was run down and an abandoned car was in the driveway. A closer look at the exterior revealed torn shades, decades of dirt on the windows, and obvious signs of a problem within. She had not been seen by the neighbors in several days, the mail was building up and the regular delivery people were unable to make contact. She was found deceased of natural causes amid what amounted to several thousand neatly bagged and crushed beer cans. She had received weekly deliveries of beer for many years, but never took cans out for curbside recycling. She just continued to pile them up to the ceiling in every first floor room. I think they filled up the entire recycling truck during cleanout operations.

Sometimes the situation is right in your own neighborhood with a person you know and you find yourself doing a combination of professional and personal interventions. This case is about a forty-five-year-old female who lived at home with her mother and held a job and drove for many years. Things started falling apart when her mom died and massive layoffs led to her job loss. She lived off her savings and benefits but was unable to find employment due to some chronic medical conditions that affected her brain and physical condition.

The local Red Cross took her as a volunteer staff member and tried to retrain her to get back into the workforce. Unfortunately, her mental problems showed that she could not keep any job. For example, she wanted someone to take her to the lavatory several times a day. When they tried to show her where it was, she said she could not remember even though it was right next to the room she was in. She finally said she did not want to continue volunteering because they did not have a lavatory! The Red Cross brought bags of food to her home where she became a recluse.

She was able to keep the house which was in her name for a few years, but then it became obvious she was struggling. Her sister in California was unable to help due to distance and being rebuffed by the client. The neighbors, Dan and Meg helped her a lot with food, lawn maintenance, snow removal, and the like. The other neighbors said she would yell out the window at them when they tried to cut the grass, and they were afraid of her even though she was all of five feet tall and a hundred pounds!

Meg tells the story of when she left her car parked on the street overnight in front of Kathy's home and received a parking ticket. The police had been called about a strange car on the street. When Meg questioned the neighbor about why she didn't recognize the car, Kathy said she only saw the left side of the car in the driveway and was viewing the right side when parked on the street and the car looked different.

The local welfare department got involved and Mary Ann and Jo Ann helped tremendously in getting her permanent disability, food stamps, and qualified for local assistance programs. One day I found her at the door black as a coal miner, with a winter coat, gloves, and hat. The oil furnace had stopped running, and she was trying to repair it when a misfire occurred and blew soot all over her and the basement. We were able to get her oil tank filled and the furnace repaired. Many times the cases go from crisis to crisis and you just persevere to keep the balls in the air and work toward a permanent solution. One day she drove to the Welfare Dept. to sign papers for assistance and complained her car wasn't steering right. We found she had driven there on three tires and one rim. The missing tire was nowhere to be found, so our mechanic jumped in to put the spare on and find a used tire.

The case went on for a few years and the Fire Department was called multiple times for welfare checks. I was usually summoned as she would not deal with anyone else and most visitors were taken aback by her unkempt appearance. She had a quirk saying "Good grief" most of the time. A throwback to Charlie Brown of Peanuts fame we think. She also had what I thought was a good supply of footwear until I opened up the thirty shoeboxes and found a lifetime of old worn out sneakers. She continued her downward spiral and eventually the welfare staff was able to place her in a group home and arrange with her sister to sell the home.

Another investigation of a senior citizen was prompted by a call from a local grocery store. This day the store owner reported the customer's skin was turning green and they were worried for his welfare. Upon visiting the house with EMS, we found the furnace was turned off for economy reasons, and he was heating himself with multiple hair dryers hooked up to a tangle of extension cords in the bedroom. His green skin was attributed to the dyes from some cheap green flannel shirts that had not been washed. We got him some heating assistance and medical evaluations that lead to placement in an assisted living facility.

Some of the hoarders can have quite a valuable collection within their homes. One particular house very ordinary from the outside with mostly original features intact from the 1920s when the house was built, contained several generations of inheritances and acquisitions. The full picture could not be appreciated in my short visit, but this was a set for "Antique Road Show." There was furniture piled everywhere and each drawer was filled. Many revolutionary and civil war era artifacts were present. The lady died and a local lawyer had arranged for an auction house to liquidate the contents and pass the proceeds to distant relatives, most of who had never kept up with this relative or appreciated her multi-million-dollar collection.

The most rewarding case in my entire career started with a complaint of bugs and nonpayment of rent from a local landlord. I gained access with the superintendent's key and found about two years' worth of mail piled up in the hallway. We had to force our way past the door and pile of mail to get in. The tenant was about fifty-six years old and recently retired as a local math teacher. There were open food containers, exercise equipment, empty drink bottles and lack of cleanliness throughout the unit. There were bugs flying all over and more on the screens looking to get in for a free meal. She had some skin issues, mobility problems, and appeared mentally weak. Her estranged mother and sister were out of state and of no help.

This person had been a career teacher who started out life as a model and had the pictures to prove it. She began showing personality issues midway into her teaching career and was shuffled around the district until she got to age fifty-five when they pensioned her off. I was able to connect with her, and we started a cleanup schedule and worked on sorting her mail.

We tried to get medical evaluations, but she resisted these attempts and had even stopped driving or going out. All her meals were delivered from local stores and delis. Several months of team efforts resulted in getting her pension payments and medical benefits reinstated. That was before the days of direct deposit and the state assumed she was dead when checks were not cashed and inquiries went unanswered. Getting her benefits restored became a key element in the rest of her rehabilitation. Some of the monies went out quickly to settle creditor liens against her checking account.

The progress crawls along, and we are starting to get frustrated. We have a hospital ready to evaluate her if we can get her admitted. Another teacher who knew her somehow convinced her to make a trip to the emergency room for the skin condition. Our connections at the hospital and the help of the social worker got her admitted for a forty-eight-hour psychiatric evaluation. At last progress!

I had to go visit the facility to ensure her staying there longer if needed. Somehow I sold my position as her advocate to the supervisor over the intercom and was admitted into the locked ward. The movie *One Flew Over the Cuckoo's Nest* came to mind when I found her running the show and shouting orders to the staff. We talked and she agreed to cooperate and get more testing done.

The CAT scan revealed a benign brain tumor that had likely been there for many years. Successful surgery and recovery returned her to levels not seen in years. Her handwriting returned to "school teacher perfect." She handled her own finances and had her driver's license reinstated. She began living a normal life again. A group of caring and compassionate people, each with a different skill, persevered to help restore this lady's life.

The biggest thrill for me was bumping into her at the local supermarket and introducing my wife to her. Dianne said the person she heard so much about over the past months had disappeared and a lovely person was now among us. I was choked up and barely able to speak. This is success.

The story ends about three years later with her death at home. She had other underlying medical conditions from years of smoking and poor nutrition. My wife and I attended her services at a local cemetery with a few friends and her family. A folding chair was set with a poster from her modeling days on display. After a brief service, her cremation ashes were distributed on the ground when a gust of wind blew them onto our shoes and pants. May she rest in peace.

Just remember that you are in a position to help someone many times in your life. Jump in and use your favors, resources, monies, friends, agencies, and anyone else that can assist you with your project. Our country is a great place with many opportunities and resources. Mental illness, sickness, family tragedies, and just bad breaks can shortchange the best of people. That person may be right in your neighborhood, so keep your eyes and ears peeled. The rewards are satisfying, and if every person helped just one person or family in their life, the world would be a better place.

5

Smoke Alarms

Things That Go Beep In The Night

There is no dispute that properly installed, working smoke alarms have saved many lives. Most of the press releases state: "No Working Smoke Alarms or Detectors Failed to Alert Residents." What about all the times a smoke alarm did alert the occupants to escape? The technology that has evolved over the last several decades detects smoke and alerts us to escape before the smoke accumulates to a deadly level. The first smoke alarm was patented in 1890 by Francis Upton, a colleague of Thomas Edison. Walter Jaeger invented the ionization chamber in 1930 while searching for a way to detect poison gases for the military. The chamber was found to be superior for smoke detection, but still no mass production. Around 1965, Duane Pearsall Company made the first battery powered detector, but it was 1975 before the Statitrol Corporation marketed smoke alarms for the home.

First, a little semantics. Smoke alarm and smoke detector are used interchangeably. Technically, a smoke alarm detects smoke and activates a built in sounder, while a smoke detector is a device attached to a fire alarm system that has a separate circuit for audible tones. Either way, the goal is to get devices into a building that will alert occupants about the early stages of fire and if possible, also alert the fire department automatically.

My collection of fire memorabilia includes some early efforts at detection devices. One is a horn mounted atop a can of pressurized gas that has a melt away link that activates the device when the high temperature is reached. Another is a wind-up gong with a fusible disc that pops off and allows the clapper to bang away until the spring runs down.

I have seen pneumatic systems that run small capillary type tubing connected to diaphragms in a control panel that activate alarms when heat expands the air within the tubing. There are also rate of rise and various button, disc, and pop off heat detectors. These were all good attempts at fire detection, but only from heat activation and only if the device was near the origin area. Most fire fatalities are from smoke inhalation, not burning to death, so technology advanced and we now have photo-electric and ionization type smoke detectors, beam detectors, along with fixed temperature devices.

The different types of smoke detectors use components that detect smoldering fires faster than quick burning fires and that technology will be endlessly debated. The goal is to have working smoke detectors properly located that are tested at least once a month. Every device installed should be recognized by Underwriters Laboratories (UL) and National Fire Protection Association (NFPA) the two biggest names in fire safety. The manufacturer's installation guide included with each unit must be read, understood, and followed.

Devices have a ten-year life span according to testing certification and should be replaced when out of date. There should be a date stamp on the back or base of alarm should you have to prove to the owner how time flies and a trip to the store is needed to purchase new smoke alarms.

The earlier smoke alarms had special batteries that were hard to find and expensive. Some were wired to plug into the nearest electrical outlet. Then nine volt and AA batteries were used. These batteries always went bad in the middle of the night it seemed or somebody needed the battery for a toy or remote control. Poorly placed devices caused nuisance alarms and the batteries were removed and protection was lost. Finally sealed ten-year battery life detectors were introduced and that solved at least the power problem.

Now we have to get the devices mounted in the proper place. I have seen many an alarm placed on furniture, mounted on a small nail, installed with double-faced tape or Velcro. Many a device has fallen on my head when testing them, another sign of poor installation. The installation has to be secure and according to directions or it will not be there when needed. I am still amazed when I visit homes that have never had a smoke alarm! What value do these people have on life? They say "I'll never have a fire" or "The fire will wake me up." They need to wake up now! There is still so much fire safety education to do, lives to be saved, and injuries to be prevented.

We adopted a policy in our department that all homes we visit will be left with at least one working smoke alarm. We carry batteries, new detectors, and tools to meet that goal. We have given away batteries, new detectors, and even offered installation free of charge. There are many grant programs and benefactors that can help fund these programs. The best policy to follow in terms of longevity is ten years discard and replace the device. Some will argue that a detector will work well past that ten-year period. That may be so under ideal conditions and even pushing the test button sounds the alarm.

How many people vacuum the detector, dust it, test it, or do any other maintenance? Does grease build up or cigarette smoke residues prevent proper function? Has someone painted the device to match the decor? Has the device fallen from the ceiling and been put back together properly, or is it damaged?

I have seen many smoke conditions where the old alarm failed to activate in spite of a new battery and the big button test. Why would you not want the best device and newest technology to protect you and your family? We spend hundreds on new cell phones and portable electronics, but cheap out on fifty dollars' worth of new fire alarms. The new ones even start to chirp after ten years to be sure you replace it.

There are also battery-powered smoke alarms that can talk to each other wirelessly, giving you an inexpensive system that can protect a modest size, multi-level home. Home centers and big box stores are a good source with many models to choose from. They often have multipacks, discounts, and product displays. So what is the excuse for not having several fire safety devices?

An alarm system from a licensed alarm company can provide full protection, alert the fire department, provide intrusion detection, monitor for water and carbon monoxide, and even alert you of ambient low temperatures. These systems can also be programmed to talk, wake up the soundest sleeper, and give instructions on your escape plan. Some of the systems can be controlled and monitored through your portable electronic devices.

Placement of the devices is critical to their function. One battery-powered device on every level is the bare minimum for most local fire codes. There should be a detector in every bedroom as well, especially if you sleep with the door closed, as this door may block the alarm sound or keep smoke in your room. Fires occur in bedrooms from smoking, electrical malfunctions, pet habitats, hair dryer misuse, mascara heating, hot wax machines, fire play, improper extension cords, and the list keeps going.

When doing renovations to a home and increasing the square footage, most building codes call for a hardwired, battery backup, interconnected system with a device on every level and in every bedroom. You would be shocked how many people spend fifty to two hundred thousand dollars on a renovation and then fight you on putting an eight-hundred-dollar fire alarm system in place.

A few other observations on smoke alarms you should be aware of. Be sure device is matched to the location, i.e., kitchen, sleeping area, basement, garage, unheated or high heat area, moist, dusty, or egress hall- way. The built-in escape lights are good to have for a hall- way unit. Avoid dead air spaces when mounting device. These can occur in room corners and on vaulted ceilings. These spaces prevent smoke from getting into the detection chamber, as there is no air flow into the device.

Testing of smoke alarms and systems should occur whenever you visit a home. The battery-powered devices can be checked with a can of spray smoke designed to test the circuits and not leave any residue. Always check with occupants before testing and be sure no one is asleep and that pets and infants are protected from the high-pitched tones.

When doing acceptance tests on a new system, try to have an alarm technician on site to assist. This would be a good time to have all the features of the system explained so that you are current in your knowledge of these installations. These systems may have addressable devices, dual sensors, and alarm confirmation circuit. Always be sure that you have control of the system and are able to silence and reset the system. Nothing says amateur worse than a blaring alarm that cannot be shut off.

For systems that are monitored by a central station, always call your dispatch center and let them know you are testing a fire system and give the address. I used to take the technician's word that the system was on "test," but after fire apparatus showed up a few times, I now trust no one. You do not want unnecessary dispatch of vehicles for all the obvious reasons: they could have an accident, they may be needed elsewhere, wasted fuel, you could be interrupting training or meals, and it just makes you look unprofessional.

When you are in any building with a fire system, a quick glance at the remote keypad or panel can indicate that the system is in "ready" status or has a fault of some type. I have commonly seen systems that were in alarm mode and had been silenced by someone, so now the fire protection system is compromised and not functioning for who knows how long. Phone lines and power get shut off in rental properties, putting the entire building and business at risk. Arsonists can also take advantage of this fire protection interruption.

I recall one tragic fire that resulted in two deaths and one severe burn injury. The fire occurred around two a.m. during a really cold two-week period. The call was from a monitoring center reporting fire detector activation in a single family home. The first due company arrived to find fire blowing out the front door and the elderly homeowner outside, severely burned and telling them his wife was an invalid and that she and the health care aide were still inside. The fire was intense, weather severe and logistically hard to access on a dead end street. The wife was removed from a rear first floor bedroom and resuscitation efforts were attempted. The aide was found later beneath a second floor window. Both had succumbed to the fire.

The house was an ice cube for several weeks, delaying the investigation by the many agencies and insurance companies. The double loss of life and severe burn injury led to prolonged litigation lasting almost eight years and targeting many defendants. The company that owned the alarm monitoring division was mostly faulted for the delayed transmission of the signal either from the home or during the relay to the municipal fire dispatch. There may have been some attempt to call the homeowner first, which also delayed the dispatch process. There were oxygen cylinders and other medical equipment present in the home that were also heavily scrutinized.

Some jurisdictions level a penalty for repeated false alarms and this is why some owners opt to have the alarm monitoring company call them first to see if there is an actual fire. I have never agreed with these policies, you are delaying dispatch and possibly keeping the people from evacuating the structure. You should instead work with the owners and alarm companies to install and maintain quality systems that protect life and property. Insist that your dispatch is notified first or at least simultaneously. You can always slow the fire response if it turns out to be a false alarm.

Document every fire investigation and be sure the smoke alarm section is thoroughly filled out. The progress we have made toward reducing smoke-related fire deaths is commendable, but there is more to be done, and we have to know how people are reacting to alarm activations and if the technology is working in the best possible way.

Our aging population and more at-home care means we have to educate people about better smoke detection and egress concerns for those with limited mobility. When you see that motorized scooter, walker, cane, or stair lift, you should think about how that family will deal with a fire and the many escape issues. There are smoke alarms with built-in strobes that can help alert people with hearing loss.

Many grandparents have sleepovers for their relatives who may not have familiarity with the house. Make some safety suggestions, upgrade their smoke alarms, and encourage fire drills in the home. Keep those public information articles supporting smoke alarms flowing year round, not just in October during Fire Prevention Week.

6

Stormy Weather: Give Me Shelter

Power Loss, Live Wire Dangers, Lightning, And More

There are many related areas of study that can help you be a standout in the fire service. Mechanical skills, construction, leadership, medical, environmental, driving, math, communications are among the top books and courses that will help you immensely in this very difficult, competitive, and unpredictable field. One other area worth understanding is weather, its terminology, and the effects on fire cause, emergency response, planning, recovery, and your personal safety. Wind, snow, rain, sun, heat, cold, and lightning are all weather components that can make for a really bad day.

When talking about weather, climate change has to be part of the conversation. Global warming has caused our storms to be stronger and harder to predict. I have noticed since 1992 that severe storms are more frequent and the sizes of the storms are off the charts. How many "storms of the century" have occurred in the last two decades? How many new weather terms have you heard for the first time?

How have FEMA and other disaster agencies seen their workload increase? How much money is being spent on disaster preparedness, recovery, and mitigation projects? The weather changes are obvious, and we must plan for the effects year round, both professionally and personally.

The marketing of weather has been a source of jokes and entertainment to us as competing weather persons strive to get it right. Computer models, farmer's almanacs, specialists, and celebrities all make for quite a show some days and even when they are totally wrong, no one gets fired. Talk about job security! I admit to being a Weather Channel fanatic.

Weather watches and warnings issued by the National Weather Service, Weather Underground, and all the local forecasters have undoubtedly saved lives and property. The naming of storms, which used to be limited to hurricanes is probably a good idea to get people onboard with weather advisories. Handheld or vehicle mounted electronic devices with weather apps, including radar, are good technology to have in the field. I'll resort to the old-fashioned method of going outside and feeling the air, looking at cloud types, temperatures, and wind direction to make my own local prediction.

The discussions on the weather websites are good to read and will help you understand terminology and forecasting variables. A "weather watcher" must be part of a successful emergency response organization, be it fire, police, EMS, OEM, military, American Red Cross, or a support agency.

Let us start by looking at wind and the effects, ranging from a few wind pruned branches off a tree, to a town wiped off the map. Wind will also have an effect on your fire suppression activities. The wind direction (always say from origin it is blowing from, i.e., out of the West) and speed will determine where you place your apparatus, command center, staging areas, personnel, and hose lines. You should always know the prevailing winds for your response areas, yet realize that storms can totally reverse the winds and this change should be a big part of your observations before, during, and after a storm.

You should understand the terms windward and leeward, so you can decide and communicate where venting should occur during a structure fire. Getting it right means the difference between a fire being stopped in the structure or area of origin or spreading across a whole neighborhood.

Wind will also cause much damage on its own. Tornadoes, hurricanes, severe thunderstorms, straight line winds can all generate winds in excess of 50 mph, which will down tree limbs and trees, scatter debris, and make driving hazardous. The downed trees may damage power and communication lines, structures, cars, and people. Roads and other access routes may be blocked and detours will extend your response times and take you into unfamiliar areas. GPS navigation may be unreliable due to storm interference and lack of current road closings.

Your OEM command center will be a key coordinator of all road data coming in from field units. Some units may be cut off from headquarters or may have to be assigned by quadrants due to road closures. Bridges may have wind issues and your higher profile vehicles will be prohibited.

Just because your truck is red with fancy gold leaf and lettering, don't think for a minute that you're immune to any severe weather. The officer and chauffeur have an obligation to keep the vehicle and crew safe and in service. Always treat any power line as energized and don't park under any large trees when positioning your apparatus. Large hail may shatter windshields and lights.

I have responded to several tree limbs downed into occupied vehicles with injuries and used to won- der what the odds were for a person to be driving by the exact spot where a tree limb would hit them.

Well, one beautiful spring day with a light breeze, a Bradford Pear sent a limb into the hood and windshield of my vehicle, covering me with glass. I never saw it coming, just a sudden windshield full of white flowers and then bam! Fortunately, my sunglasses and Subaru protected me from injury. The SUV was damaged to the tune of $6,000 and now had a blemish on its car history. Now I think of all the storms I've driven through over the years and never gotten a scratch on me or my department vehicle.

Straight line winds (SLWs) are a phenomenon that I have seen several times and *wow* was there a lot of damage! Unlike a tornado that spins, causes circular damage, and has its own wind scale, SLWs can come out of any severe thunderstorm, especially microbursts. The heavy rains that occur in a more tropical type severe storm push the winds that are aloft toward the surface. These winds then line up and blow in one direction and cause severe tree and structure damage. All the trees fall and the wind takes a path across an area, so people think tornado, but it is different because all the trees fall in one direction.

The two SLW events I witnessed were two to four miles in destruction length and a really straight beeline on the map. Mutual aid companies that came to assist say they saw no damages until our town border and the next town to our east that had much less severe damage. Many enormous trees, some over 150 years old, were toppled onto cars, houses, streets, and power lines. Many streets were closed for days and power interrupted for several more days. We tried for a FEMA declaration but were denied for being too localized, so private insurance and our local budgets had to absorb the entire cost.

I did get to see the after effects of a small tornado in my town. The sun was out and beautiful on the west side of our three square mile town. On the east side near the Passaic River, we got reports of a storm and all kinds of damage. The path started near some commercial buildings in the town to our south, damaging some roofs, continued along River Road and took down some trees and telephone poles. Then it took a right turn across State Highway 21 where it flipped an eighteen-wheeler over and then crossed the river to knock down about forty trees in a county park and then dissipated.

When I called for additional resources, no one could believe the storm had even happened! The utility company had no other calls, so they swarmed the area with equipment and manpower, restoring power in record time. The shelter the bosses insisted on opening went unused, people stayed to watch the action, and guard their homes. The weather service would not say it was a tornado because no one called them to investigate. I am quite sure it was an F-0 funnel cloud based on witnesses, the irregular hopping damage path and the circular damages.

Several other wind events have been predicted with better accuracy because they were associated with hurricanes or winter storms. My observations are that any storm coming from the south or northeast in my town would be bad. Either direction does not have the mountains and other topography to break up the storm's strength, so lots of rain, snow, and wind. A storm from the south brings flooding tropical moisture and a nor'easter brings snowy ocean moisture.

These storms and winds have caused power and communication outages lasting for several days and even into two weeks in isolated neighborhoods. We never saw outages lasting past twenty-four hours in the past, so this also tells us that we have more severe storms and must plan for this.

A large number of people installed natural gas and diesel powered standby generators for their homes and businesses. More people have purchased small portable generators and various solar-powered gadgets to power their electronics and small electrical loads in their homes. The need for heat and air conditioning, medical conditions, food preservation, and our ever increasing reliance on electric will continue this trend.

Pay attention to locating your portable generator, as they create carbon monoxide, a colorless, odorless gas that can kill you. Never operate a generator in a building or garage and position them at least twenty feet from a window or doorway. Read your owner's manual and understand how temporary electrical cords need to be connected. Store fuel in approved containers and in safe locations. Permanent stand-by generators require installation permits and utility approval.

Most fireplace gas inserts are now sold "storm ready" so you can get some heat if the power goes out. The cell phone sites and Internet providers have all installed backup power supplies. The utilities have stepped up their tree pruning schedules and invested in storm preparedness. The alarm companies have also made changes to implement longer battery life and wireless communicators to ensure fire alarms, panic alarms, and intrusion detection all continue to function during storms.

You too must invest so that when the big, bad wolf tries to blow down your house, you and your family will survive. Trim dead and diseased trees, check your roof, repair all windows, have tarps handy, install a generator, have a self-powered cooking area outside, stockpile food and water, have several coolers available, clear your yard before a big storm, lower your awnings and umbrellas each night, have flashlights and batteries, have a plan for power outages, have a disaster drill with your loved ones, and of course, keep an ear to the weather.

One local woman, the wife of an army veteran, took drills very seriously. She would run surprise fire drills at two in the morning and all four children would leave the house and report to their meeting spot across the street.

One time a power failure affected a paraplegic who was very dependent on his motorized wheelchair for getting around the apartment and to evacuate if an emergency occurred. My friend Joey Bee and I secured a generator and ran an extension cord up to the second floor apartment. We were able to supply electric to his wheelchair battery charger and the television so he could be both mobile and informed on the local disaster.

Thinking back to my youth, I do remember getting the first ergonomic, Teflon snow shovel for Christmas and using it often to make a few bucks and get some exercise. Snow blowers were only owned by wealthy people or large property owners and usually would not start due to lack of use and disrepair.

Sometimes several years between big storms would pass, the gas would go stale, starter ropes would break, and rubber parts would dry out.

Today, many people own snow blowers ranging from small electric blowers to large 10 or 15 hp double or triple stage snow throwers. Now some of these purchases can be blamed on an aging and unfit population or the lack of teenagers looking to shovel, but the need for snow removal equipment is greater than it has ever been.

Global warming or climate change does not mean warmer always, but it does lead to more extremes in weather patterns. Remember the 2015–2016 mild winter interrupted by an historic blizzard dumping thirty inches of snow on the northeast? My forty-year-old snow thrower worked overtime on that storm!

Planning for snowstorms is essential to ensure that your town is ready for both the early season slippery one incher and the two feet of crippling wet snow. Resources that must be in place include snow removal equipment, road salt, tire chains, fuel supplies, new windshield wipers, snow brushes, ice scrapers, shovels, hydrant markers, hydrant maps, or GPS hydrant locator, sand, and contractors.

Roads must be kept passable for EMS, police, fire, DPW, and sanitation trucks. The command center should have direct contact with the snow plow supervisor so that a lead snow plow can be dispatched to clear the way for an emergency response vehicle. All vehicles should have a shovel that can be used for digging out a vehicle, clearing a fire hydrant, or shoveling a path to the front door.

There will be plenty of calls for cars that get stuck and rescues of stranded motorists, so have blankets and shelter areas available. Heavy snowfalls can lead to collapse of weak buildings, car ports, awnings, sheds, and other lightweight structures, so be sure you are up to date on confined space and collapse rescue techniques.

Some calls will be from homeowners who cannot open their door due to the snow and a simple dig out visit solves the issue. Your locality should have some type of senior or disabled assistance program that identifies invalids and others who will always need help. The Nutley program was called SOS for Shovel Out Seniors. This program can be staffed with volunteers, teenagers, church groups, service organizations, and neighbors. Run press releases to remind people to "adopt" their closest fire hydrant and clear the snow from around it.

There are times when Mother Nature will throw you a curve ball such as the "Snowtober" storm that hit in 2011. In early October, with leaves still on the trees, a freak snow storm deposited wet, cement-like snow on the northeast and caused wide spread tree and shrub destruction. Branches started snapping everywhere taking down power lines, damaging cars, buildings, and blocking roadways. Being outside was the scariest event I have ever seen or heard, as branch after branch kept cracking with gunshot-like sounds and you could not zero in on the direction because there was so much happening at one time. The debris cleanup went on for months and the tree companies had plenty of work into the winter months, normally a slow time spent sharpening saws. My four-inch diameter birch tree bent all the way to the ground from the weight, but somehow survived thanks to my frantic snow and branch removal efforts.

I am always amazed by the rush to the store for supplies before a big snowstorm. People should have food, water, and disaster supplies in stock at all times. Put a seasonal press release in the local paper and on websites reminding people to prepare. Medications, personal supplies, and other necessities should never run lower than a fourteen-day supply. Consult Red Cross and FEMA websites for suggestions on preparedness and become a "prepper." Remember when storms hit, you may be working a double shift or unable to get home, so be sure your family is disaster ready.

Polar vortexes, wind chills, subzero, snow, sleet, freezing temperatures, blizzards, bomb cyclones and other conditions associated with cold weather extremes can really make us miserable. Dressing in layers, with the wicking layer closest to your skin is imperative. Good high-tech gloves, hats, scarves, hoods, socks, and goggles should all be part of your cold weather ensemble. Extremities must be protected from frostbite or you could lose a finger or toe. The very least may be a lifetime of cold sensitivity in your hands or feet. Wet clothes will also add to your chills and make it very hard to warm up. Keep your feet dry with good boots and thermal or wicking layers of socks. Uncontrolled shivering can indicate hypothermia and the need to take warm-up actions. Hypothermia can lead to loss of muscle control, slurring of words, fatigue, coma, and even death. Soups and broths are good ways to warm up and hydrate. Observe wind chill warnings and be sure to limit your exposure time.

The misery of frozen hydrants, frozen hoses and couplings, frozen sidewalks, ice-covered apparatus and turn out gear, broken water mains, and piles of snow all make the case for cold weather planning. Have a salt truck on call to help prevent slips and falls when your suppression water freezes everywhere. Traction mats for the pump operator are worth purchasing. Keep a pail of sand on each rig to create a safe step zone around your apparatus. Crew rotation is imperative to help prevent injuries and ensure everyone gets home safe.

The laws we have to enact really drive home the point that people have not been trained or are too lazy to deal with snow. We have to tell you to clear your sidewalk within forty-eight hours. We have to declare snow emergencies and tell you to stay off the road unless you are an essential employee, which the majority of people are not. We have to tell you to clean off your vehicle windows and roof before venturing out onto the road. We have to tell you not to park on snow covered streets so the plows can get through. We have to tell you not to throw the snow from your sidewalks into the street. Some towns want to level a fine if you don't clear the snow from the fire hydrant in front of your house. Be a good neighbor and follow the rules, especially clearing off your vehicle, so you don't injure or kill the person behind you. Helping an elderly or disabled neighbor will earn you a special place in heaven, and you will feel good assisting a fellow human being. Be sure your children are made aware that helping family and neighbors is part of being a good citizen.

When we think of lightning, the first thought people have is Ben Franklin attaching a key to a kite and flying it into a thunderstorm to prove lightning was electrical in nature. Ben was a thinker and planner who studied and found solutions for many issues of the day, both practical and political. He organized the first fire suppression brigade in Philadelphia in 1736. His well-known phrase "an ounce of prevention is worth a pound of cure" actually refers to fire service activities.

The study of lightning is called fulminology and many aspects of this phenomenon are still not completely understood. What we do know is that it can be five times as hot as the sun's surface. A bolt is about as wide as your thumb. Lightning strikes occur about forty to fifty times a second around the globe. Lightning can strike more than once in a location. Fatal lightning strikes in the U.S. average fifty-one annually. A person has a one in 960,000 chance of being struck by lightning in the U.S., better than winning the lottery!

There are three main types of lightning: cloud to cloud, intra cloud, and cloud to ground. The last, cloud to ground is the most studied and will have the biggest impact, as the strike will impact people, structures, and vegetation. Fear of lightning is called astraphobia and there is no shame in having this fear; it's dangerous stuff!

There can be direct strikes, which is what the term implies. There can be adjacent strikes, which will cause indirect damage, but still be lethal. The best policy is not to be out in a thunderstorm if at all possible. There can be "bolts out of the blue" if conditions are just right. Should you be able to hear thunder, which is the result of the air turbulence, you can be struck, so take cover.

Many sports fields have installed lightning detection systems, which will give early warnings of impending danger. Personal sized lightning detectors are also available. Heed these warnings immediately! Should you be around water, such as pool, lake, ocean, or on a boat, take cover on land and spread the word of any storm warnings you know about. The time between a flash and the thunder report can be measured in seconds to help determine how far the storm is from your location. This is called the flash to boom ratio. For every five seconds you count after a flash of lightning before the thunderclap, the storm is one mile away. There is a good lightning safety video on JOEYBEE.TV that covers all this information.

Brick or other solid structures will protect you the best, just stay away from the windows, which should be closed. A metal topped car may protect you with its mass, not the rubber tires being insulators. Stay away from tall objects such as trees, flagpoles, chimneys, etc., as these can be struck more easily due to the path to ground the object provides. Talking on the landline phone is still discouraged as a direct hit on a telephone pole nearby could bypass the lightning arrestors in the circuit and harm you. Lightning rods or building protection systems are available but may or may not work as designed, due to the lack of maintenance generally seen on the wires, connections, ground rods, and other components.

In the event you are out in the storm away from shelter, take cover in a low lying area not prone to flash flooding and make yourself a "basketball with feet" and hands over your ears. Do not lie down in a ditch, as this puts more of your body in contact with the ground, which makes you a better conductor of electrical charges. Cover your ears because if the strike is close, the thunderclap can be deafening and cause hearing loss. Should your hair stand on end, a strike is near.

I have seen many fires caused by lightning strikes and in most cases damage was severe and just a matter of bad luck. One storm, which came out of the south, was so severe with flooding rains and frequent lightning that our calls came in one after the other. A power transmission line was hit and fell to the ground arcing across from a gas station where they were still pumping gas! Hit that emergency cut off paddle button as soon as you arrive. The roads were flash flooding in five minutes making travel treacherous. Thunderclaps were super loud and immediately after the flash, like a military barrage. A pole was struck and a neighbor saw the energy travel along the wires to an unoccupied home that we forced entry to and found the bed on fire next to an outlet. Many home electrical panels and transformers in that neighborhood were "fried." We had at least a dozen fire alarm panels that sent false signals to our dispatch center. The storm formed right over us and without any warnings. I love thunderstorm shows, but that one was scary and did a lot of damage.

Another storm that centered over a valley in town, just five blocks from fire headquarters, did a number on a traffic signal, some school computers, and started a fire in an occupied home. The occupant reported sparks shooting out of the wall outlets and smoke in the home. We found a stubborn basement fire and fire operations caused a lot of damage to the home. During our investigations, we found a blow out in the foundation where the strike had found a path to ground and ignited the wood structure inside. The electrical service to the house had a temporary connection and a probable improper grounding circuit. The storm we watched from five blocks away did not seem very severe and this fire was the only run we had that day.

We have seen plenty of telephone poles damaged by strikes. Trees blown apart when the sap is superheated and the tree explodes. Gutters have been blown off houses by strikes. Chimneys have been collapsed or damaged by strikes. Many investigations were to assure residents that the nearby strike did not damage their homes or businesses. Keep in the back of your head, not to lean against metal fences or stand on metal edged curbs, as these could be conductors of electric looking to bite your butt.

Temperature extremes are also weather phenomenon that must be planned for. Extreme heat will dehydrate and exhaust your crews. Plenty of water, cooling misters, air conditioned rehab areas, tents, crew rotation, and shade are all components of good crew safety. Understand heat indexes and know that once they are above eighty-five or ninety degrees, steps must be taken to protect the troops. Heat indexes are computed using temperature and humidity, so you will hear it is eighty degrees but feels like ninety. The body will be less able to cool itself through sweating because evaporation will not occur.

You should monitor your urine year-round. Winter dehydration is very common due to the thirst and sweat signals being absent. Dark urine indicates dehydration and straw-colored urine indicates fluid intakes are good.

Kidney stones can cause cola-colored urine from the blood being excreted as the stone cuts up your urinary system. My kidney stone happened during the winter due to excessive sweating from snow shoveling, working on my new house and using cola sodas and coffee to stay awake. I don't care what women say, passing a stone has to be worse than delivering a baby.

Use caution with sports drinks as they contain a lot of sugar and can overwork your pancreas. Dilute sport drinks with water if you use them. You should drink before getting thirsty as this is an early signal for dehydration. Cracked lips are also a sign of the need for more water. Ice water will rehydrate your body the quickest.

Heat exhaustion is the first stage of overheating. Sweating, fatigue, elevated body temperature, cramps, headache, paleness, nausea, and skin that is moist and cool are some of the signs that a person must cool down and hydrate.

Heat stroke is when the body is way overheated and has stopped sweating. Extreme fatigue, mental confusion, heart irregularities, rapid pulse, seizures, vomiting, coma, and elevated core temperature are signs of this very dangerous, life-threatening condition. You must cool this person immediately or brain damage, organ damage, and even death can occur. Ice packs under the arms, in the groin, and around the neck are good areas to cool the veins and arteries. This person will need IVs of cold saline to hydrate and cool the body.

Back during my EMS days, we had a friend who ran a 5K race without much preparation or experience. He only knew how to focus and extend himself through martial arts training. He ran the race as hard as he could and was in heat exhaustion by the end and bordering on heat stroke. We took him to the emergency room for treatment. While there, he became violent and had to be restrained. His fear of needles and mental confusion compounded to make a bad situation even worse. Eventually, he was cooled down and returned to normal balance.

Another extreme heat event occurred at our Junior Olympics program one really sunny hot day in June. Five grammar schools sent their fifth and sixth graders to our sports complex to compete in various events to see which school had the best athletes. The student spectators sat in open bleachers from about 10:00 a.m. until 12:30 p.m. The children and their teachers did not prepare for the sun. No hats, water, sunblock, sunglasses, or other items were thought of as they left home for school that morning. The blazing sun started taking effect on the athletes first and then the crowd. They started dropping like flies, and it was threatening to turn into a mass casualty event. The diabetic students were moved to shade and air conditioning first, they being the most at risk.

The nurse and EMS crews worked quickly to triage the affected students, and I summoned the fire department to set up a cooling shower. We filled buckets with ice water along with towels and torn sheets so we could place ice cold compresses on their necks. I was most appalled at the disarray of the blood testing kits that the diabetic students had and the lack of good sun sense by all. Everyone was fine by the time we moved to a shady picnic grove. The same type of event occurred at high school graduation a few years later and several adults were treated for heat exhaustion.

Many times you may be dealing with special needs children and adults. A person that is known to them during heat stress or other events may help to control the situation and restore their balance.

A crossing guard was reporting about a mother with an out-of-control son on a hot day. I was in the area and stopped to help. A special needs student from the local Phoenix Center missed his bus and the mother was determined to get him to school to maintain his continuity with lessons. She took several commuter buses in the heat and by the time she got to Nutley, the boy was way out of control both physically and mentally. We got him into the shade and gave him some water and tried to encourage him to go three more blocks with us to school. We also called the school to advise them of the situation. The principal, Dr. Doug, drove over and within one minute calmed the child, put him in the car, and took the child off to school. This center is a special place with an awesome staff that attends to dozens of special needs students that no other facility is equipped to handle. Our autism rates and the number of special needs people are still rising, so read some books, audit a special needs class, take a course, and develop contacts with these specially trained educators.

These hot temperatures can contribute to fire dangers including brush fires, spontaneous combustion in barns and attics, overheated vehicles, and overworked HVAC units. Drought will often accompany heat extremes, so be sure your water supply is available. Fire hydrants may be opened in neighborhoods for children to cool off, lowering available water main pressures. Drafting points may be unusable due to ponds or rivers being lower or dry. Wells may run dry from water starved aquifers. Invest in a cooler to carry water and ice on your rig.

More personal and family storm preparedness should include a "go bag" containing clothes, food, water, identification, medicines, personal care items, spare cell phone battery or charger, flashlight, cash and other items that would be helpful during a short notice evacuation. The Red Cross and FEMA have suggestion lists on their websites.

Your personal information should also be protected from damage and copies stored in a separate location. This can include birth certificates, marriage license, divorce decrees, tax returns, bank account numbers, health insurance, life insurance policies, car titles, driver's license, credit cards, Social Security card, passport, phone numbers, and address for friends, family and businesses, computer passwords are all good things to have available to reestablish your identity and make claims for losses.

You can buy water and fireproof safes for documents and other items that need protection in your home or office. Banks have safe deposit boxes. Family or friends out of your immediate vicinity may take in your information packets. Cloud, disks, or other such digital storage can be another way of accomplishing preservation of documents. Whatever way you decide, take action now, as storms and other calamities will not wait for you to get prepared. These steps can also help families during untimely deaths and disabilities as they attempt to put their lives back together again.

These are some of my storm stories. You, your family, and crews will experience many storms. Prepare for all types of events and keep an "eye to the sky."

7

Water, Water Everywhere

Flash Floods, Rivers & Streams

Rain is another aspect of weather that can adversely affect fire calls and cause wide spread catastrophic damage. From little April showers to drenching, soaking rains that go on for days or weeks, water has to be part of your planning. Those little misty showers after a dry spell can lead to power line failures. The carbon tracking on the pole insulators does not get washed away quickly enough and electric takes the wrong path to ground and can cause high voltage lines to arc and then drop to the ground from a break in the wire. These 10k lines or larger are always spectacular as they dance, spark, and arc about the ground. Hopefully no people, cars, or buildings are nearby.

Always protect back at least three utility poles and watch metal curbing and fencing that may be con- ducting current. These wires can appear to be dead sometimes as circuit breakers open and close, but don't be fooled and never approach downed wires without expert counsel from the utility company. Protect your eyes from flashes and arcs, which are bright and can damage your retinas just like welding does. Hot sticks, insulating gloves, and insulating mats should only be used by the well trained and only if the equipment is maintained and tested.

I have had a few experiences with utility personnel and prefer the ones with a little gray in their temples, just like airplane pilots. One time a tree had damaged a transformer and the feed line. Our tree trimmers per policy waited for the lineman to declare the line safe to work near. However, a trimmed branch fell toward the wires and arced, tripping the street circuit breaker. We were quite upset with utility's answer. "Now it's really safe. We'll reset the breaker after you are done."

Another incident involved a smoking transformer pit on the main street. Fire crews waited for utility response, and we were told repair work would begin and everything was safe. After fire crews returned to headquarters, a large explosion with flames and power failure occurred. We responded back to secure the area and hoped no one was dead or injured. We found the lineman had gone down to inspect the transformer and found the cooling oil boiling, so he scrambled to get out, just before the explosion occurred. The resulting fire endangered the entire underground electric grid, almost leading to a network fire. A shopping carriage full of groceries was left behind on the sidewalk when that shopper ran home to change their underwear.

They later found a lightning strike nearby that had occurred several days earlier caused damages not identified during previous repairs. After much consulting and many supervisors appeared, we sup- pressed the fire with foam. What a training video that would have been! The utility called several times to see if we had located any videos, but this was before the widespread use of surveillance cameras.

Pay special attention to utility workers during large storm events. The crews may be working doubles and be exhausted. Mutual aid utility workers from several states away may be working on unfamiliar equipment and certainly be in unfamiliar areas. I recall seeing Florida Power and Light working in New Jersey after one of our "storms of the century." Overall, the quality and commitment to safety is terrific and management ensures quick, but safe operations.

Rain events can cause flash flooding, mudslides, road collapse, tree uprooting, basement flooding, and road closures. These effects can be devastating to a large area. Any rivers, be they tributaries, small streams or large waterways can rise quickly and cut off neighborhoods, strand cars, wash out bridges, and make responses very difficult, if not impossible. Know your district's flood map and which areas will be high impact needing special attention. Fast water rescue teams, road barriers, signs, high wheeled vehicles, high boots, life jackets, boats, pumps, generators, mops, water vacuums, etc., should all be part of your flood fighting arsenal.

Climate change and construction have come together to cause larger floods and create water problems in previously dry areas. The large trees that are one hundred years old or more are being lost to construction projects and building owner's fear of damages. These monster trees drank lots of water, up to one hundred gallons an hour, and stabilized our soils. Rains have become much more torrential in nature and for longer duration.

The "paving of paradise" or creating impervious surfaces is making for much more storm runoff that overloads our storm sewers and the rivers they discharge into. Quick responding streams and flash flooding can catch everyone off guard. Vermont had only about four to seven inches of rain from Hurricane Irene but had catastrophic bridge and road damage, with some areas isolated from travel for a week or more. This is a state with many trees and unpaved areas, but the mountains shed the water into the gorges and valleys, moving boulders, rerouting rivers, and wiping out homes. Restoration work went on for years and flood mitigation plans have been designed, but who can really know if they will work?

We all know of homeowners who never had water in their basement in fifty years now having dewatering systems costing thousands of dollars. French drains, dual pressure systems, sump pits, or whatever term you use have become big business to protect our basements that are now living space, contain our furnaces and laundry, or used to store all kinds of possessions.

The biggest thing to remember is to test the pumps and other components so you know they will work when the big one hits. Pour a bucket of water into the pit and make sure the system is functioning as designed. Think about power failure time and design a generator, or water powered back-up pump into the system.

Be sure the discharge is to the outside and well away from the building, so you do not pump the same water. Never discharge your sump pump into a sink or sanitary line. This is a code violation and can lead to overloading the sanitary lines and causing sewage backup into your home or the person's downhill. The sewage authority also has to deal with this excess water and bill your locality. You guessed it, this leads to higher taxes.

Many times we will find one house in the middle of a hill has water in the basement and downhill they have none. Blocked gutters, improper downspout discharge, poorly pitched driveways and sidewalks, and neighbors' discharge can all contribute to a wet basement.

Never take the floor sanitary sewer cap off to drain the basement. Pressure can cause sewage back flow into the home and you could lose the cap in the resulting excitement. Basement toilets can present a problem during times of sewer system reversals. I have seen twelve-inch high geysers out of toilets with no way to correct it during the height of the storm. You can try putting a bowling ball with a blanket around it into the toilet bowl to control low pressure flows. Another family had a large plunger and took turns holding it in place inside the commode.

Back flow or check valves can be installed in problem neighborhoods, but they will require frequent maintenance. One owner put a submarine-sized shut off valve in place after years of back- ups. Good thing to have, but only if you are home to close it and remember not to flush your toilets when it is closed.

Remember to protect you and your crew from raw sewage and its many unhealthy effects. Hepatitis, viruses, critters, and chemicals will all be present and can cause immediate and long-term health issues. Bleaching and other decontamination methods for your gear and equipment are mandatory. Respirators designed for such use or self-contained breathing apparatus (SCBAs) are needed to protect your respiratory system. Disposable suits, boots, and gloves are also good supplies to have on hand. A Haz-Mat team or private clean-up contractor will also be very valuable to your operation. These events require more than a bottle of hand sanitizer and turn out gear.

Electrical hazards in flooded basements will be present. Outlets, extension cords, and circuit panels can energize the storm water and lead to electrocution. Do not assume the circuit breakers have tripped or the power is off. I have seen many circuit breakers still operating underneath five feet of river water and the only solution was to cut power to the building from outside.

Gas leaks can occur when pilot lights are submerged and extinguished and the safety valve fails to stop the flow of gas. Shut the main gas valve if water is impacting fuel-burning appliances in the basement or anywhere else. Most modern furnaces and water heaters have electronic ignition these days, so this is less of an issue. The drawback to the solid state and ceramic style burners is, once wet, they are junk, no more drying them out for a few days and relighting.

Heavy rains and blocked roof gutters on flat roofs can cause building collapse and severe water damages inside the building. Keep in mind that water on a roof can easily exceed the designed load especially if snow, acting like a sponge, is also involved. Sometimes you get a warning if the rooftop skylight or bulkhead door is letting in water. Recon from an adjoining building or other elevated position and evacuate the building immediately. These roof drains must be inspected frequently.

People can do amazingly stupid things when driving during heavy rains. Most people don't think to pull over during a really heavy downpour and just keep speeding and hydroplaning along without good visibility until they lose control completely.

Driving through flooded roads has always been an indicator of poor judgment. I have seen people drive around barricades and right into two and three feet of water and many times the detour was only one block! Some days it looked like demolition derby as many cars were lined up, disabled in the water. Just because your GPS device says, "Go that way," use a little common sense. The pickup truck or SUV that just crossed the water sits high off the ground and has higher motor components that may be somewhat water resistant.

Your little car with the energy efficient under carriage will now act as a boat and float you toward death. Even if you go slowly through shallow water, the driver coming the other way could care less about the wake he is sending toward your car. The police started to really crack down and gave out obstructing the roadway summons to these bad drivers and had the tow company remove and impound the vehicles. Most vehicles that suffer this fate are not repairable due to water-soaked electronics and water in the engine cylinders. Remember the Scottish proverb, "Don't wade the river if you can't see the bottom."

We had one lady whose car was swept away at night into the main stream, and she somehow self-rescued herself onto a tree until the water subsided and then knocked on someone's door the next morning. Another young student drove her SUV into window height water and stalled. We rescued her with a big wheeled front loader, and she asked if we could tow her vehicle out of the water so she could get home. When we told her the leased truck was most likely totaled, she burst into tears. Another motorist was attempting to turn around and ended up driving into the stream and being swept away. Fortunately, it was daylight and witnesses alerted some firefighters who just happened to be nearby. They made a spectacular barehanded grab at the bridge and saved her life.

The phrase "turn around, don't drown" still needs some more marketing. Motorists need to heed barricades and emergency responder's directions. I had one guy flip me off and proceed through a flooded roadway. The detour was one block. He did make it through the water, but the police car on the other side promptly wrote him up for disregarding a traffic control person, and he had an expired registration. Karma can be a great thing!

The manhole covers or sewer grates can be lifted by the water pressure and these open holes can break an axle or swallow up a person. Sightseers can be hard to control, and they may not see these missing covers or where the sidewalks end. Kids riding their bikes through the water are another headache for response personnel. Bullhorns or PA systems can be helpful to call out to people at the other side of the water hazard.

One big rescue event took place early in my career on the Rescue Squad and had tragedy, com- plications, resuscitation, and a spectacular technical rescue. A report came in for two kids stranded in a tree in the park by high water. Police, fire, and Department of Public Works (DPW) staff started a rescue operation with little equipment and training, but lots of bravery. Men started jumping in the water, and three were swept away by the fast current. One DPW worker was floating face down when I arrived and a number of us were chasing him looking for a rescue vantage spot.

A DPW worker in front of me collapsed face down in the water and had no pulse or breathing. My first witnessed cardiac arrest and our equipment was a block away, so I sent a young boy back to alert the other EMS workers. This was 1975 so no AEDs, paramedics, or other such advanced equipment was around. A pericardial thump was used to try and restart the heart. We started using an oxygen demand valve and commenced CPR but were unable to restart him. His nephew drove the Cadillac ambulance to the hospital and another soaking wet police officer was put in the rig with us. This officer had been swept under the bridge along with his partner and came out the other side to shore. His partner was unaccounted for at this time, but he became a bigger part of the story as you will read. The floating DPW worker was grabbed from the water by some firemen, given mouth to mouth, and was revived. That DPW worker returned to work and achieved retirement.

Many rescue teams from both municipalities and private industries were converging on the site. A shoe was found, family members and everyone else showing up suspected the worst. Then someone felt pounding on the bridge pavement. The missing officer was under the bridge in an air pocket! Rains had subsided, so the river had crested, but water was still at bridge level. Dive teams could not make access due to extreme current in the river, so a plan was made to create an access hole through the bridge deck. The town engineer did a quick mark out, jackhammers were brought in to break up the cement and the Public Safety Commissioner said, "Dig." Rebar was struck at some level, so we put the scissor cutters on our Hurst Jaws of Life (tool #3). As luck would have it, one of the hydraulic fittings malfunctioned, so a cutting torch was used instead to cut the steel bars. The officer was lifted out of the hole to the cheers of hundreds of rescuers and spectators!

One fatality and three "saves" that day made for media coverage, lots of commendations, and one field promotion to sergeant for the trapped officer. Nutley's Third River, a small, picturesque tributary of the Passaic River, can morph into a raging monster and will continue to present rescue and flooding concerns far into the future.

This is a scenario that brought national attention due to the use of a psychic that happened to reside in Nutley. Sunday morning December 3, 1967, five-year-old Michael Kurcsics went out to play with his seven-year-old brother. Around 8:15 a.m., Michael fell into the Third River that was swollen from snow melt. His brother tried to rescue him but was unable to grasp his hand. Michael was swept away and drowned. Rescuers using dive equipment, boats, grappling hooks, and even an amphibious car could not locate his body. Two hours before his accident, local self-proclaimed psychic Dorothy Allison awoke from a nightmare that predicted Michael's death. She saw him in a number of other visions. Allison went to the police, described the clothes Michael was wearing, which was not public information. Allison also began seeing the number 120 and 8 and saw his body found behind a school. She added more clues such as the parking lot behind an ITT factory, lumber, and gold lettering on a window. Investigators believed that the number 120 might have been an address or the date January 20, but they were still unable to locate Michael.

On February 7, 1968, Michael's body was found and the main investigator on the case was told the news at 1:20 p.m., the same number that kept coming up in Allison's predictions. Michael's body was found near Elementary PS 8 on the riverbank across the street from a lumberyard, next door to an office building with gold lettering on the window. Directly across the river was an ITT factory with a parking lot. Michael was wearing the same clothing as Dorothy described.

Allison was used by the police as a consultant in five thousand cases worldwide including the Patty Hearst kidnapping and Son of Sam investigation before her death in 1999. I met her husband Bob back around 2008 when he was involved in a traffic accident. No one at the scene recognized the name or was aware of his wife's activities. We talked for a while, and I gave him a ride home, savoring on the way, all his stories from a time already forgotten.

Tropical Storm Floyd in 1999 was my Waterloo. This storm was the remnants of a hurricane and was massive in size covering large portions of the Eastern seaboard. There was decent forecasting of a major history making flood and no way would it go out to sea. The rains started early and kept up nonstop throughout the day and by 5:00 p.m. things were quite saturated and the rivers were exceeding their banks. Then it really started to rain as hard as I have ever seen it come down.

Our radio communications were disrupted. Roads started to flood further back than normal, cutting off all but two cross-town streets. People were trying to get home and kept getting detoured adding to frustrations and dangers. People were walking through flood waters up to their knees, unaware of missing manhole covers and eroded riverbanks. A bridge collapsed severing a ten-inch natural gas main. Hundreds of houses and businesses started taking on water. We rescued several dozen motorists from stranded cars. Storm totals were over fifteen inches!

Many homes had to have their utilities shut off, and we evacuated several neighborhoods that had become new river routes. We used CAT front loaders to access these high water areas and put the residents, including a ninety-year-old woman, in the bucket for their trip to high ground. Parents became concerned for a group of students working at the local grocery store. Water was rising around the store and bags of cat litter and dog food were being used for makeshift sandbags. We rolled up with the CAT and scooped up the screaming girls and took them to high ground. I appointed one boyfriend as transportation coordinator to arrange for trips home.

Pumping requests came in for weeks, and it was hard to accommodate everyone. Additional pumps were hard to purchase due to a region wide demand. Somehow, the electric stayed on so those who had permanent pumps or garden pumps were able to keep up with the water. Many neighbors banded together to purchase, borrow, and help each other pump. The sanitary system was overloaded and the elevated sewer access points went underwater causing a reversal of the sewers in parts of the town. The tide was in, so our tributary that empties into the Passaic River backed up until the tide went out allowing the town to drain. Many trees, debris, sewage, fuel, and yard furniture floated downstream, destroying foot bridges, bike paths, landscaping, playground equipment, and anything else in its path.

No one was prepared for the ten-thousand-gallon underground fuel tank that was now an above ground fuel tank. We had been removing all our underground tanks at the township garage and this particular one had been pumped dry of fuel to prepare it for removal. The power of groundwater hydraulics took care of the excavation step and sold me on the folly of underground storage tanks being installed in flood zones.

One of our best kept buildings, a sixty-unit apartment complex, is located adjacent to our stream, and they took in over six feet of water in the basement. The electric stayed on somehow and the evacuation was voluntary. The heat was not needed, and hot water was not available for a while. The fire alarm panel shorted out causing the hallway fire gongs to sound. The only way to fix this was to ride the CAT to a balcony access point and enter the hallways to unbolt the bells. We put up some temporary smoke alarms to provide some protection until the system could be repaired. This undoubtedly contributed to my gray hair conversion.

My partner, future Captain Thomas Nicolette, was with me during this time and was instrumental in helping many victims and me. My wife was calling to tell me water was coming in through the basement walls, and I had to come home. We had moved a lot of furniture into the basement on Tuesday in anticipation of having fifty people over for a couple's club party we had committed to six months earlier. Now on Thursday we had to move this furniture back upstairs and deal with four inches of water on the floor.

Remember the comments I made previously about making your home and family disaster ready because you may not be able to get home? Thanks to my Dad and brother Robert who came over to help wet vacuum and mop up the basement. The party went on as planned, but without the use of our waterlogged backyard.

On a personal level, this was the most demanding disaster I have ever experienced. I was awake thirty-six hours straight and it took over six months to get my sleeping schedule normalized. I felt like a zombie for much of this time and totally stressed out. I have photos from some family events, and I look really bad in them. I probably should have gotten some medical screening to find out if all the sewage I had been exposed to was causing issues.

A great friend and mental health counselor Bob Mc Donald helped me a lot with some advice and coping methods. He felt I took on everybody's problems as my own and was being overwhelmed with the sheer volume of issues. I think my vitamin regimen and good eating habits, along with my generally good health got me through this period, but did cause more gray hair.

The town's damages included eight pedestrian bridges destroyed, sections of gabion walls washed away, bike paths washed out, buildings damaged, supplies destroyed, debris removal, overtime expenses, fences destroyed, mold removal, pump repairs, fuel depot repairs, trees and soil lost from parkland, and offices destroyed.

The last words I have on this memorable storm are about damage claims that were my responsibility as damage assessment coordinator on our OEM staff. I would get to deal with township insurance companies and FEMA to try and recoup over five hundred thousand dollars in damages and labor expenses. Now I am sure you have all done some type of insurance claims, so you know how much red tape there is. Multiply that by a hundred and do this on top of having to do your regular workload at the same time. We did thirty-seven separate project worksheets.

This would use all my organizational skills, accounting knowledge, negotiation skills, and all the favors I had accumulated through the years. Claim and restoration work went on through June of 2000 and small details continued for another year before closing out the FEMA files.

The help each department supplied was fantastic and I could not have finished without their help. Leonardo da Vinci Vespucci, Harry Kirk, Rosemary Costa, Mike Luzzi, Jack Barry, Kathy Ritacco, Bob Searle, Marie Viccarello, John Holland, many appraisers, FEMA reps from all over the country, Filomena Coldebella, Tom Pandolfi, and countless others all worked together to restore the township both physically and financially. FEMA has stream- lined their process since then and provides much more local assistance in filling out their ever changing claim forms.

Flooding issues seem to be in the news more than ever. Climate change, El Niño cycles, overbuilding, and deforestation will continue during our lifetimes and rains will become more frequent and catastrophic. Floods and water issues must be part of your preparedness plan both personally and professionally.

8

Fireworks

Sparkly Things That Fly And Go Boom May Kill You

Imagine spending over eight hundred million dollars for something that self-destructs, makes loud noise, creates litter, causes injuries, and you do it every year as a way to celebrate. The fireworks market has exploded (pun intended) over the last several decades into a bottomless pit of marketing and spending of our hard earned money and limited tax dollars. Call me a party-pooper, but I never quite understood the fascination with loud noise, crowds, fire, and injuries that accompany our declaration of freedom, sporting events, new year's, and other celebrations. The laws pertaining to fireworks are as varied as our states are and thankfully the larger displays have Federal regulations that apply. I have worked many a municipal show, broken up many small illegal shows, and taken educational courses run by our State Division of Fire Safety, so I do have a lot to say on the subject.

The injuries alone should be enough to deter amateur use. People lose eyes, hearing, fingers, hands, and suffer painful burns from sparklers, firecrackers, roman candles, little tanks, and other small, seemingly harmless items. The bigger fireworks, M-80s, ash cans, mortars, and the like also cause property damages that can be both accidental and intentional.

I recall one licensed vendor doing a church celebration with two-inch mortars firing "reports." He was missing several fingers and had a scarred face from many incidents over the years. We were certain to keep a good safety zone, wore our turnout gear, and used a tree for cover. We still got hit in the arm with a misfired shell piece, but thankfully did not incur any injury. We told the sponsors that he would not be returning next year. To add insult to an almost injury, I was subpoenaed to his hometown Municipal Court as a defense witness. While he was in town shooting the show his pack of wild dogs escaped their enclosure and attacked a child. The prosecutor inferred that it was an intentional release and proceeded to have him found guilty and fined without any testimony from me. There was an obvious dislike for this citizen with a history of uncontrolled dogs. No defense lawyer would have been successful.

Overseeing a municipal or other properly permitted show can be quite challenging, as the details are many and any omission could lead to property damage, injury, or even death. I think most of my gray hairs have come from twenty-five years of working July 4 and church pyrotechnic shows.

One must start with interviewing the vendors and having a site meeting to ensure launch site spacing to crowds and occupied buildings meets code. The laws say sixty feet for every inch of shell, but one hundred feet gives you a little more safety cushion. Think about the two-inch shell going two hundred feet sideways toward people instead of straight up. You must also establish a security perimeter and be able to maintain it for several hours during set-up and during actual firing of the show. This has to include everyone not in safety gear: police, firefighters, politicians, family, and friends of the technicians or anyone else who thinks they are privileged. No one ever looks down a mortar tube, *ever!*

When the shells arrive in that rented truck with the little tiny placard and the racks are being set up, the location is closed to everyone, period. One year the crew was tying some ground displays to a chain link fence that were to be electronically fired. The power box had not been discharged properly and a static charge went down the line and fired off the whole fence load. Fortunately, the crew was unharmed, and we had maintained our security zone so no civilians or staff members were injured, just shaken up. They are all now believers in my firm safety rules.

The technicians with larger companies are licensed and receive training, but low bidder rules can come into play and then watch out for the part-time/seasonal lead person with a bunch of trainees. One such crew, all two of them, showed up one year about three hours late to get the show loaded. They had to construct the mortar racks, load the shells, wire the fuses, have dinner, and read the boss's memos. They arrived about 5:00 p.m. with one set of pliers, one hammer, one wire stripper, and about one-half of the contracted shells. The mayor and deputy chief got really anxious when I kept telling them the show would not be ready by 9:15 p.m., the customary time. Finally, after much screaming and threats, the show was fired at about 9:45 p.m., and what shells we had, went up without any issues.

When I think back to the first shows early in my career and prior to Federal Law changes, I marvel that we never really hurt anyone or damaged structures. The show had eight, ten, and twelve-inch shells fired from steel pipes behind the high school back stop and about 75 feet from the crowd! There were no preloaded racks or battery fired displays. Load each shell, light it with a flare, and reload the next shell as quick as possible. We laddered many municipal buildings looking for hot embers on our high school, library, and town hall roofs. Wind direction meant either lots of ladder work or lots of eyes being flushed out in the crowd by our EMS group.

People still lament that the old shows had better percussion on their chests, was louder, more multiple reports, and larger spreads of light. Maybe so, but the danger was not worth the risk, and I feel displays are viewed better at a greater distance.

My wife, Dianne, liked to attend the municipal shows and always was on the lookout for the best vantage point for viewing. One year the firefighters suggested she climb the fire truck and lay on the hose bed to get the best view in town. Well she enjoyed the show, but that white shirt and pink pants she was wearing were covered in ashes and never the same again.

The weather plays a large part the day of your show. The time to set up a show safely has to be five to six hours ahead of launch time for an average small to medium show. This means if you have a 9:00 p.m. show time then you must consult with everyone by 3:00 p.m. You should continually view your weather report for rain or excessive winds and decide if you have to call a postponement that will not incur financial penalty and allow ample time to notify the public of the date change. A small passing shower may not be reason to postpone, but you have to be sure the vendor is ready to cover the racks and fuses with plastic or tarps of some sort. These really humid nights can also lead to shells getting hung up in the mortar tubes, so watch out for rack explosions or low altitude shell ignition.

Do not run toward any racks that are on fire or misfiring. That is the technician's job. Your main job is to be sure that the agreed upon launch diagram is followed and the racks are inspected and secure before the shells are loaded. Two nails per rack cleats and no broken tubes. A rack that falls over or points in the wrong direction can lead to a cascade of bad events. One year the vendor was straightening bent nails to have enough for his nailing schedule. This is a sure sign of low bidder and poor business model.

We had public shows at several locations in town trying to find the perfect spot for crowd access and safety, security perimeter, bathrooms, artificial lighting that we could control, building separation, fire truck/EMS access, street closures, and vendor access. Artificial turf became a new concern and forced us to abandon sites that worked well. The insurance underwriters also kept us on our toes and the local airports had to be notified of schedules. These were long, hot work days from about 1:00 p.m. until 11:00 p.m., so water, food, rehab, spare radio batteries, ear protection, big flashlights, and our own safety became a ritual for us every year. The administrative side, even though we started in January, always seemed to run up to the last minute.

We ended up back at the traditional beloved downtown location when the new "cake box" shows started to be used. These were several dozen boxes with six hundred small tubes in each that were wired together and mixed up with many special effects that were pretty and loud, yet met code for crowd separation. The only drawback is the total litter mess that needs to be cleaned up after this type of display (600 tubes × 40 boxes = 24,000).

Be sure and pick a parking lot or street area so mechanized equipment can be brought in to help. The post show ground sweep is mandatory to look for duds or unexploded shells. You don't want anyone to pick up a shell the next day and try to light it off. The vendors usually have a good idea of any misfires and will help you. Do not pick up any shells or look down any mortar tubes! These are large events requiring a strong command organization that is focused on the safety of thousands of people. Be sure that each division of your structure communicates with each other and works toward a safe, successful event.

The intent of public shows, be they government or privately sponsored, is to have an event that will satisfy people's need for sight and sound and discourage home and other shows run by untrained people. Many ethnic groups have a culture that embraces these family run displays that injure people every year and cause lots of property damage. Alcohol and recreational drug use also play a part in impairing people's judgment and reaction time. The thinking that I'll be able to get out of the way of a misfire is a fallacy. One cannot react fast enough to an errant rocket or shell. The impact on children's and pet's hearing need to be thought about also.

This class of fireworks is mostly manufactured in faraway lands with no safety or manufacturing protocols. The companies and the people who sell these explosives are strictly out to make a profit and could care less about your safety. Most people wrongly store their firework stash in plastic bags where a static charge could build up and cause detonation.

The personal financial exposure that people incur amazes me to no end. Who is going to pay if someone gets injured or killed? Who is going to pay for a new house or vehicle destroyed by fireworks? How would you sleep at night if someone gets maimed or handicapped for life? We have seen many cases of fireworks stored in bedrooms and other living areas in the home just waiting for a spark or other ignition source to cause a conflagration in the building.

Think about the firefighters who have to enter that home for fire suppression activities and now have one more uncontrolled event happening. I remember one raid on a teenager's home who was selling fireworks to his friends. We found his room with a full display area worth several thousand dollars. The mom said she was unaware of these fireworks in the son's room, talk about enabling.

Some of our patrol activities involved juveniles in possession of fireworks, some just "playing," and others being quite destructive, blowing up playground equipment, water fountains, toilets, bridges, windshields, and mailboxes. We found a house party with drunks firing bottle rockets into a neighboring gas station. There was the eighty-year-old man tossing cherry bombs into the street eleven o'clock at night.

There was the neighbor who was firing two-inch mortars in the street, fifty feet from a church, and his own home and with children watching from fifteen feet away. I spoke with him, trying not to embarrass him in front of the kids, asked for his stash and got quite an attitude from him in spite of the wife taking my side. I ended up charging him and going to court where he gave the judge a hard time and not surprisingly, ended up with the maximum fine under a local ordinance. On his way across the parking lot, he gave us the one-finger salute and muttered some choice words. No father of the year award going his way.

Many times we would find parents lighting off fireworks very near children and their own homes. Another neighbor was firing bottle rockets into my friend's yard and swimming pool. I spoke with them but did not take their fireworks at that time. Several weeks later, the kids were playing with sparklers and the sparks got too hot, causing the kid to fling the sparkler toward a very expensive evergreen tree, turning it into a roman candle requiring fire department response. Now I took their fireworks without any comment. Karma is a great thing.

Model rockets are a related area of concern. Many go quite far up or sideways during a failed launch and once ignited you can't take it back or control it. One such model rocket ended up in a school bus parked next to a school building and totaled the vehicle with the ensuing fire. We found the rocket kit in the parking lot, but no one around. The alert custodian had seen the mother drop the kids off and copied down the license plate. We worked out an agreement with the families and their homeowner's insurance to reimburse the school for their children's transgressions. Amazingly, the parents asked if they could have the rocket kit back from our evidence room. We did not honor their request and our shocked faces must have made them rethink their demand.

The Internet has created a whole new issue with homemade devices and recipes that anyone with a computer can research. We had one such group of adolescents going to a store and buying cleaning products, aluminum foil, and two-liter soda bottles. The dopey clerk must have thought these kids were ambitious and making a few bucks cleaning homes. What they were doing was mixing these over-the-counter products and putting the foil into the soda bottle and quickly capping the plastic bottle and running. The chemical reaction and resulting explosion was quite impressive as one went off when we were approaching from our surveillance positions.

We rounded up the gang and called their parents, thankful that none of them got sprayed or blinded by the chemicals when the bottles exploded. We endured some abuse from a few of the parents who thought we were overreacting. Some community service hours and a three-hour Juvenile Fire

Setter Intervention seminar drove home our message that we care about your children and their safety.

Now it seems that we will be dealing with terrorists, both extremist and home grown, so any controls we can implement on fireworks could help us at least sort out noise from an attack or just some person's illegal fireworks show. Right after the September 11 attack I was able to persuade the church celebration to forgo the fireworks portion of their parade out of respect for those who died and everyone else's nerves.

Indoor pyrotechnics shows have become quite common place, upping the excitement at sporting events and nightclubs. The very tragic Station Nightclub fire in Long Island killed 100 people and injured 230. This incident shows that fire codes are ignored and that event sponsors may not care much about your safety. The incident video can be found online and the unedited version is quite graphic. Should you be at such an event, look for a fire safety permit, or safety personnel assigned to protect you. Be sure you have an exit plan and if you feel uncomfortable leave before "things hit the fan." Most fire codes call for a practice run of the indoor fireworks show to be witnessed by the fire official prior to the public being admitted. I wonder how often this rule is observed.

Another area of concern is drones. The impact of these technological advances will be great and I hope positive. I can see their use by farmers, ranchers, and rural residents to survey their vast acreages and get supplies delivered. The problems will arise when these drones are used in populated areas and near airports. Untrained, stupid, and probably bad people will create untold havoc on our airspace, violate our privacy rights, and cause injury and property damage. The drones will continue to get more powerful and have longer flight times, so a drone could be miles from where an operator is stationed. Drone registration is an attempt to control things, but like gun registration, an imperfect solution. Some type of limiting program that keeps drones out of no fly zones and other restricted space is essential to our safety. Our expectation of privacy in our own backyard is probably lost forever.

There are several educational videos at CPSC. GOV website on illegal fireworks. Jason Pierre-Paul of the NY Giants has partnered with CPSC to inform the public of the dangers and his severe injuries caused by fireworks. The annual injury count from fireworks will astound you.

If you have gotten to this point in the chapter, I thank you for taking the time to understand the inherent dangers and stupidity associated with uncontrolled fireworks use. Should you be at a party and the fireworks come out, speak with the host or leave the event if they will not stop. When you see illegal fireworks being set off in the neighborhood, call the police or fire department. You may prevent an injury or property damage, maybe even your own.

9

Fire Sprinklers Are Automated Heroes

The 24-7 Automatic Firefighter

This is a chapter that will explore the facts and myths of fire sprinklers. No fire person worth their salt will dispute the safety and effectiveness of having sprinklers everywhere possible. Sprinklers in the home, workplace, high-rise towers, and places of assembly will all be explored and the case for installation will be indisputable. The fire service must continue the battle against developers, investors, code officials, politicians, and design professionals who want to save a buck at the expense of people and buildings. The sprinkler coalitions, sprinkler fitters, fire chiefs, NFPA, and other fire service supporters must remain strong and unwavering in their efforts to market and install sprinkler systems.

First, let's dispel some myths. Forget movies and television shows that feature large discharges of water from a sprinkler system. This is strictly for effect, as are the scenes of firefighters rescuing people and fighting fires without SCBAs and other basic safety equipment. The average sprinkler activation of a correctly designed system is one to four heads. The water damages from sprinkler systems are far less than a fire hose discharging 100 to 200 gallons per minute after it has been dragged through the building to reach the fire area.

A common misconception is that sprinklers will raise your insurance rates due to water damage potential; this is untrue and in fact, they will lower your rates. Think structure damage, business interruption, injury and death lawsuits, inventory and contents loss, which will all be reduced by the installation of sprinklers. Sprinklers are not expensive to install when done as part of a construction project when the walls and chases are open for piping the systems. The uses of CPVC and PEX systems under NFPA 13R designs have dramatically reduced manpower and time expenses. Remember to focus on the positives, because most people will focus on the negatives based on their misconceptions.

Sprinkler installation in new construction is specified in model codes that are in effect for your state or jurisdiction. The only wide spread exemption is for one and two family homes where we have the greatest loss of lives and the most injuries! We must keep on lobbying to change this unacceptable situation.

There has been a movement on partial systems in homes using plastic water lines connected at various points to the domestic water lines. These would be used in high fire incident areas such as kitchens and basements, as well as protecting the egress paths of the home. This, in my opinion, caves to the anti-sprinkler interests.

A full sprinkler system with a water flow alarm is the correct way to protect one and two family homes and their occupants. The codes will mandate the types of buildings, areas, and occupancies that require sprinklers, but don't be afraid to ask for them to be installed voluntarily. Have your sales pitch ready and cite some incidents where sprinklers worked. All they can do is say no and then this puts you in an "I told you so" position should a fire occur. This may sound aggressive, but we have been fighting a losing battle for many decades and have to ratchet up the effort if we want to convert the sprinkler opposition.

Another term you should know is "retrofit." This means modifying an existing building to make it safer for the occupants and attempts to correct overlooked systems that can enhance the structure's performance during a fire event. These retrofit positions come out of responsive legislation that results from loss of life or large destructive fires. Some examples are high rise structures that never had sprinklers and relied on fire departments climbing from seven to over fifty stories, wearing gear, humping hose and tools, and then having the stamina to fight a fire on multiple floors.

The Meridian Plaza Fire in 1991 is a good study case for retrofitting high rises. The building was a thirty-eight-story office building built in 1972. The fire started on the twenty-second floor in some discarded linseed oil rags and progressed up to the thirtieth floor despite intense fire suppression efforts. The fire went to twelve alarms and burned for almost twenty-four hours. Engineers feared for a building collapse as the steel structure members were exposed to the heat, so firefighters were withdrawn, but not before three firefighters died.

Finally, on the thirtieth floor a retrofitted sprinkler system stopped the fire's progression. A total of ten sprinkler heads kept the fire in check, but not before eight floors had been damaged by fire. The building was never able to fully recover and was demolished in 1999. Most states have enacted a retrofit law for high-rise buildings over seven stories. These buildings should never have been constructed without a fire sprinkler system, but at least now we can make the change for safety of the occupants and firefighters.

The Seton Hall University Dorm fire in 2000 resulted in three student deaths and fifty injuries. A relatively small bulletin board and sofa fire in a building with no sprinklers and a history of numerous false fire alarms and compromised compartmentalization features all came together for that "perfect storm." New Jersey Division of Fire Safety promptly enacted legislation to mandate on-campus dorms and assembly buildings were to be retrofitted with fire sprinklers.

Off-campus buildings are not as strictly regulated, so tragedies will still occur. Other states and countries have not followed through on changing the sprinkler laws, so be sure to ask about fire protection features if you or a loved one are going to school and staying in a dorm or unregulated housing. Church affiliated schools may also be allowed exemptions or long periods of compliance due to financial concerns and successful lobbyists.

There are several types of fire sprinkler systems. The most common is a **wet system** that takes the water from either a dedicated or shared water main and directs it through risers, branches, drops, and sprinkler heads appropriate for the area being protected. These are used in heated buildings and warm climates. Special freeze protected sprinkler heads and specially engineered insulated adapters can be added to protect parts that may be subject to freezing, such as a balcony, freezer box, or lobby. Components that complete the system include outside stem and yoke valves (OS&Y), back flow preventers, branch valves, alarm flow valves, main drain valves, and Fire Department Connections (FDC).

Dry systems are a method used to cover areas subject to freezing temperatures, such as truss lofts, attics, parking garages, and loading docks. Here the piping system is filled with air and held to sixty or so pounds of pressure with an electric jockey pump. When the sprinkler head fuses or opens due to fire, the air rushes out and the clapper valve opens to let water flow into the pipes. These systems can be expensive and do require maintenance. Be sure the jockey pump is located in an area where the noise from it cycling won't create a nuisance.

A cousin of dry systems is the **pre-action system**. This system also uses air to ensure the system is ready. Fire detection is accomplished with smoke, heat, or other detectors that trip open the water valve and fill the system with water that waits for a sprinkler head to open and extinguish the fire. These systems are used in high value areas, computer centers, electrical rooms, libraries, museums, and other areas were water damage needs to be limited. The detector trip should also be reporting to a monitoring station with the theory that the fire department intervenes before the water starts to flow out of the system. Systems will usually be made with galvanized pipe to limit corrosion in the system.

Anti-freeze systems are another way to deal with cold areas. Premixed glycol solutions are put into the pipes, and this ensures integrity of the system. When the sprinkler head opens, the glycol empties out the open head(s) and allows water to enter the system to complete the fire sprinkler operational matrix.

The last is a **deluge system** that can be used to cover a high risk area where a quick response is needed to extinguish a fire. These could be in a loading dock or storage area and operation can be attained through manual activation or detectors of various types. All the sprinkler heads would be opened and operating simultaneously, hence a deluge of water.

Whatever system is installed be certain that licensed design professionals, local water utility, and installers are included. These are not do-it-yourself projects and even licensed plumbers may not have the experience in all the new components and procedures on the market. I was lucky to have an industrial complex in town that had every type of sprinkler system that exists, with union sprinkler fitters installing them and on-premises engineering oversight. The sprinkler fitters, supervisors, and management are all highly trained and very willing to share their knowledge with you. Take advantage of these resources and work along with them so you can learn about new technology and know that the work you are inspecting is code compliant.

You must take some courses in the various nuances of sprinklers and know the NFPA 13 code sections, mechanical code, plumbing code, and building codes. This chapter is not written to make you an expert in sprinkler installation, just to whet your appetite and encourage your participation in sprinkler advocacy.

A sprinkler system's life span can be amazingly long. We have had hundred-year-old systems with some routine maintenance, waiting to extinguish a fire after all those years of standing guard. One particular system functioned many times, including an arson fire involving a jacket, a dumpster fire against the building window, a rack fire among some plastics, and another arson fire among some merchandise. Another seventy-five-year-old system protected convention displays and one night while closed, a fire on the workbench was extinguished by one sprinkler head. Another occupancy produced printed circuit boards and the heaters on the acid baths would malfunction and set the plastic tubs on fire. Every time the sprinklers worked and saved the building from catastrophic destruction. The last sprinkler activation was in a retrofitted five-story apartment building. The tenant had left a decorative fireplace with improper gel fuel containers burning. The fireplace surround caught fire and one sidewall sprinkler head extinguished the fire.

This brings me to another area of discussion on fire sprinkler systems. When doing plan review for large big box stores, be sure in-rack sprinklers are designed into the fire protection plan. These stores have revolving and seasonal inventory, some of which can be flammable or highly combustible, so you must design for the most severe fire load when calculating water flows. These buildings will have wide open floor plans and lightweight steel bar joist holding up the roof. Early collapse and difficult roof venting operations will be part of an uncontrolled fire that will be mostly contents.

Watch the repurposing of buildings that have sprinklers already in place. Many times the system was designed for a totally different use, and it may not be properly protected with the old fire sprinklers. We are starting to see catastrophic fires in warehouses that are "fully protected," but not at the correct level for the new occupant. This is an issue in government owned buildings that are subject to internal oversight and sublet to tenants. The water mains may not be sufficient, in disrepair or are over-taxed in the industrial park, so the system may not function as designed. Fire Prevention Bureaus and

Code Enforcement Departments must have a unified front when meeting with developers, landlords, government bureaucrats, and the like. Remember, you are supposed to be the experts and the Authority Having Jurisdiction (AHJ).

The last big "failure" of fire sprinklers was at the Avalon at Edgewater New Jersey fire in January 2015. This was a 408-unit, very large, lightweight construction apartment complex fire which burned one building to the ground and damaged an adjacent building. Plumbers had been working in a wall with a torch and started a fire, which they tried to put out without notifying 9-1-1. The fire progressed in the voids and involved the lightweight wood truss structural members. Sprinklers do not cover these concealed spaces, so the fire grew unchecked. The first arriving fire units had to deploy evacuation and rescue crews for the primary search, so the fire grew even more. The sheer volume of the structure, fast burning and failing lightweight structural members, delayed alarm, and the life safety exposure would overwhelm the largest of departments. There were over five hundred firefighters at the scene for almost twenty-four hours.

Miraculously no one was killed, so you can say the fire sprinklers did their job providing evacuation time for the occupants. The sprinkler system was not designed to save the structure. Two hundred and forty units were destroyed in this daytime fire. The ensuing discussions and investigations called for better fire separation of smaller buildings, more robust fire resistive construction and using steel pipe fire sprinkler systems, not the NFPA 13R CPVC systems that were intended for one and two family homes.

I have a cooperative builder in Nutley that listened to my sprinkler sales talk and agreed to put a dry sprinkler system in the truss lofts of the apartment buildings he was constructing. This was above and beyond the code requirements and expensive. This agreement occurred ten months before the Avalon fire. Never be bashful about negotiating. The codes are a minimum standard of compliance.

Windowless areas, especially basements, present an extreme hazard to fire suppression crews. When a fire occurs in these areas, discovery can be delayed so the fire grows unchecked. Venting procedures to allow hose line advancement can be difficult and may require special tools and knowledge. The heat, smoke, and toxic gasses accumulating in these areas are killers both to people, pets, and the building. Many insurance companies and fire codes now recognize this hazard and have called for monitored fire alarm systems and fire sprinklers to be installed retroactively. The important feature on these systems will be the Fire Department Connection (FDC) that enables the suppression crews to apply water from a safe exterior position while creating fire and smoke vent openings.

FDCs are an important design feature of sprinklers and must be suppression crew friendly. A sign calling attention to the connection is first along with a red jelly jar light over the location for twenty- four-hour visibility. Pumping pressure sign can help reduce the pump operator's stress load by posting this inlet pressure number.

The fitting should be accessible and not blocked by bushes, cars, signs, walls, or other encumbrances. The fitting should match the Fire Department's thread, be it threaded or Stortz. Be sure and check this on inspections, as I have found the wrong thread had been installed many times.

The FDC cap should be a locking one, such as Knox, to prevent tampering by vandals, arsonists, or junkies using it for a drug drop point. Be sure FDC master key is available on all rigs so the cap can be removed quickly.

The angle of the hose connection should be such that the supply hose will not kink and be easy to connect. Large diameter hose (LDH) connections may need a forty-five-degree angled fitting to ensure an easy, kink-free water flow. There are some discussions on LDH hose being used for this purpose. Some professionals feel that LDH is not an attack line and that two-and-one-half-inch supply lines should be used to feed sprinklers at all times.

Consult with your fire experts and develop a standard for use throughout your district and keep some conversion adapters on the rigs for mutual aid runs, and those Murphy's Law installations. Double female and double male adapters can be useful when the swivels on the FDC are frozen. These steps will ensure your engine company's FDC connection assignment is always successful.

The water flow valves should be monitored by a central station alarm company and provide a local interior and exterior audio/visual alarm. The tamper switches, branch valves, and air pressure switches should be monitored by a central station and provide a local trouble alarm through the main fire panel.

The last type of sprinkler system is known as a **special agent system**. These are used in locations where water would be detrimental to the equipment or reactive with the contents within the protected space. Misting systems may be used in electrical rooms and generator trailers to contain a fire but minimize damage and electrocution hazards. Be sure you pre-plan these installations with company representatives so you understand the operation of the system.

Another special agent system uses special extinguishing gases and is commonly known as an FM 200 system or clean agent system. The older gases used were halogenated compounds (halon) and relied on concentrations at a certain level in sealed rooms interrupting the chemical reaction in the fire tetrahedron. Halon was found to be damaging to the earth's ozone layer so this compound's use was discontinued. This is where the fire triangle was modified to explain the extinguishing actions of special agents. These systems are used in computer rooms, computer hosting centers and other high value areas where water, foam, powder, and fire department activities would cause catastrophic damage. These systems have a very involved operational matrix that may include an alarm with escape time, manual override delay, dual sensor activation, HVAC shutdown, alarm activation, door interlocks, dump sequence, and purge fans. Read the signs that will be in place at these installations and follow the directions. You cannot stay in the room during the dump and purge phase or you will be extinguished also. These system activations are costly and an alternate fire protection plan will have to be put in place until the system tanks are recharged.

Many times these systems can be paired with a VESDA air sniffing system that will detect the slightest combustion particles and initiate a technical response to investigate and correct the situation prior to a system discharge. These will also be high security areas protected from intruders and may require escorts, access cards or badges, eyeball scans, and mantrap interlock overrides.

The final type are **kitchen suppression systems** known as UL 300 systems, which provide fire extinguishment in an area limited to the cooking appliances and exhaust hood duct work. These systems primarily use a wet or foam agent that will work on fires in oil and vegetable fat fryers and all common cooking appliances and are mandatory on most commercial cooking operations that create grease laden vapors.

These systems should be checked and maintained once or twice a year depending on cooking volume and grease buildup. Systems will have an operational matrix that can be initiated with either a manual pull station or a fusible link. Features include a gas valve shut down, electrical shutdown, alarm activation, agent release, make up air shutdown, and an automatic temperature probe to turn on exhaust fan.

There should also be a Class K manual fire extinguisher nearby that can be used in the event system activation does not control the fire. The system activation must be done first so the fuel source is shut off and fan operation continues to carry the extinguishing agent into the plenum and duct work.

The biggest problems with such systems occur when the owners install new appliances or move equipment so the protection nozzles or the tank size are now not protecting the modified area properly. Installation approvals for new systems with the contractor will include a full matrix operational test with balloons on the nozzles and an air tank put in place of the foam tank. Put on your eye protection and have the cook pull the handle then watch the show as the balloons fill with air and pop while you check the entire matrix for function. I always try to have the kitchen help pull the activation handle because they will be the ones present during a fire and probably causing the problem.

These cooking suppression systems have given us a little entertainment from time to time with accidental releases of the foam. One very large system that had slaved together six smaller systems all discharged at once in a local industry's cafeteria. The service technician was blamed for not checking the fans or cleaning properly so the fusible link melted and activated the system. No hot meals that day in the lunchroom.

Another technician was allowed to service a suppression system in a catering hall three hours before a holiday party. The control cable was wound too tight. It came apart and the system activated. Foam was everywhere, and it contaminated the prepared food, forcing the owner to call off a party for eighty-five people on one-hour notice. The Grinch really stole Christmas that day.

You can see that there are many methods to protect people and equipment from fire using various fire sprinkler or fire suppression systems. Be sure and document all sprinkler activations in your NFIRS reports and submit local press releases when you have a good save from the fire sprinklers. We must continue to market the importance of fire sprinklers in every type of structure and lobby for code changes. Whether you are building, working, traveling, or just out having a good time, fire sprinkler systems or the lack of, should be a large part of your personal fire survival plan.

10

Fire Never Takes a Holiday
From Nursery Schools To Seniors

A Plan for Educators and Fire Houses
Educational Programs for Children

The one activity that I truly enjoyed was teaching children about fire safety. This activity is also the hardest to document for success. How do you prove the lesson you taught saved a life or prevented a tragic incident? You must have an inner drive that most educators have, to know that preventing even one burn injury or one fire death makes all the effort worthwhile. A fire educator will be one of those "unsung heroes" that day after day preaches the lessons of fire safety to every child and adult they come in contact with. Ralph Waldo Emerson has been a constant source of inspiration for me throughout the years.

Success

Ralph Waldo Emerson

To laugh often and much

To win the respect of intelligent people and the affection of children

To earn the appreciation of honest critics and endure the betrayal of false friends
To appreciate beauty
To find the best in others

To leave the world a bit better, whether by a healthy child, a garden patch or a redeemed social condition
To know even one life has breathed easier because you have lived
This is to have succeeded!

When you start your outline for an educational program, be sure that you thoroughly know your topics and the curriculum. There are many prepared programs from NFPA, USFA, Shriners, local burn centers, and other professional educational groups. These lesson programs will be a good starting point and will add continuity to your presentation and provide handouts and literature to reinforce the lessons. There will also be various videos that can be shown, but do not rely on these. Electric, screens, and projectors add to the tech load and complicate your set up time. The goal is to have a simple, portable program that can be taken from school to school easily. You should have taken some instructional courses by now and carry fire instructor credentials. Public speaking comes hard to many of us, so training will make you a better presenter. Get friendly with a local educator or school principal who can mentor you.

Many schools will let you sit in the back of the room and observe veteran educators who are anxious to share their knowledge. Be ready to jump in, you may be asked to read some Dr. Seuss or give a memory or two on your school days. Fred Rogers of *Mister Rogers' Neighborhood* is a great show to watch and learn techniques that are timeless and will work for you. Calm soothing voice, eye contact, and friendly smile go a long way in connecting to your students.

Ages 3–5: Day Care/Nursery Schools

We are looking at preschool level programs in this section, not PowerPoint high school level presentations. The group wants to hear your words, personalized stories, and lessons. The program must be interactive and make learning fun. When firefighters walk into a day care classroom, they are easily recognized and are instant community heroes. You have the attention of the children for fifteen to twenty minutes, now make the most of it. The school should be contacted to schedule the visits, and they should be given a copy of the outline for approval. Some of the locations are part-time classes or AM/PM and this may require multiple visits to reach each class. The staff will select the best room for the lesson and will assist you with seating and any discipline issues. Sitting on the floor at their level always worked the best for eye contact and being accepted as a teacher and friend. Introduce yourself as a firefighter and ask the class some of the things firefighters do and if he or she is your friend. Watch out for the one who says they have something to tell you. They can have a totally unrelated story that can lead to an avalanche of narratives from the rest of the class. Take your cues from the staff for controlling the excitement and maintaining decorum.

I continue to be amazed at the level of intelligence, language grasp, and just how smart these three-to-five-year-olds can be. The early years for children are the most formative, and you have a chance to be part of this. Be ready for these human sponges. Do you remember many things you learned in preschool and kindergarten? The students go into overdrive learning after first grade and are bombarded with so many subjects and by the age of fourteen know everything. You all know adolescents that constantly say "I know that," so it must be true. Children are the most vulnerable to burns, their skin is easily damaged, they are still learning about hot things, their judgment skills are still being formed, they are just so quick to do things, and burns can take up a large percentage of a small body.

Burns can occur in so many ways: beverages, food, ovens, grills, candles, bathwater, sun, matches, lighters, fire pits, tobacco products, fireplaces, microwaves, irons, batteries, automobiles, curling irons, and electricity are all common areas of danger for children and adults. Parents have many distractions in their home life, so the skills for burn avoidance must be taught at an early age directly to the children and then be reinforced by the schools and family. Parents many times play a primary role in these injuries. The spilling of hot beverages, glorifying candles, letting children light their cigarettes, leaving matches and lighters in easy reach, improper use of pool chemicals, not establishing a "no zone" around grills and stoves, allowing lawnmower and tractor play, and just being careless on leaving hot items within reach of small children are just a few of the practices I have seen happen. Parents should take a first aid and CPR course.

The first visit to preschools should be with an engine and ladder company. Meeting the firefighters and seeing the equipment is always a winning approach. Be sure a safe location from other vehicles is selected, put out traffic cones, have children controlled by teachers, stay away from truck exhausts, and do not blow the siren or air horn with the kids nearby. We actually had a car drive into a legally parked ladder truck one time. Fortunately, no one was hurt, except for the car. This visit should be early in the school year while the weather is warm and students are adjusting to the new experience of life without parents. This also lays the groundwork for a classroom visit later in the year as students get accustomed to school life and guest speakers.

Show them the compartments, talk about the tools, and explain how the engine and ladder work. Letting them squirt the water with a booster or trash line is always fun. Have some plastic helmets to make it more fun and limit any cross contamination of head lice or other conditions. The presenter should have a bullhorn or other amplifier to ensure the class gets your message.

Have a firefighter put their gear on one piece at a time in front of everyone, with gloves and air pack being last. The firefighter should then walk among the class looking for high-fives and allow them to hear the breathing sounds and see up close what a rescuer looks like.

There may be a few children who are afraid, so let the teachers comfort them if needed. The school run by the nuns in our town had a zero tolerance for crying in class. They reminded me of Tom Hanks in *League of Their Own* saying, "There's no crying in baseball!"

Costume character heads such as Sparky the Fire Dog or Smokey Bear can add extra excitement. Just know that the rookie usually gets assigned the costume duty, so give them a quick lesson in mannerisms and approach and keep them hydrated, these costumes get hot.

Take many pictures to use in press releases and on school bulletin boards. You want the parents to see what the fire department is doing to educate their children about fire safety and hopefully they reinforce the lessons.

There are many approaches to teaching burn awareness or burn avoidance. I settled on a very simple and very portable system for our pre-school students. Called the Hot Box, it is a large plastic tote filled with various items from around the home. Toys, curling iron, ash tray (remember those), little toy bathtub, toaster, batteries, lighter, matches, baking sheet, pot, coffee mug, and any other small hot items you can find around the home. The toy items should be small, fun, unbreakable, lightweight, and easy to clean. The contents of your kit should be sanitized often to limit germ spread. You should use hand sanitizer and get your flu shot each season.

We would first talk about hot and cold and the ways you could get burned, that it would hurt and you may have to go to the doctor. The children would sit on the floor with me and take turns coming up and removing one item from the box and talking about it. Then we would put it by the hot or cold sign on either side of the box until all the items were removed.

This is a good interactive program, inexpensive, and makes learning fun. The items should be basic, easy to discern hot or cold, but be ready for that unexpected comment kids are famous for. A yo-yo could hurt you if swung around or the nun's class called a twelve-inch ruler a "hitter." You will develop your own cadence as you do this program and it can be refined for the age group.

We would then practice our crawl low in smoke drill. Discuss smoke and fire, what the effects are and how to stay low in smoke by crawling. Then two people take a blanket and hold it about two feet from the floor, waving it and having the class crawl from one side of the room to the other while staying low under the "smoke." Get one child to demonstrate the skill before the entire class does it. Again, some students may balk, so have a partner or teacher try and get them through it.

Stop, drop, and roll is another skill set that can be taught using felt practice "flames." First, explain how clothes can catch on fire and that this is the only way to practice. Have a demonstrator come up as the felt flames are stuck to their clothes and then start the drill, having them cover their faces with their hands and rolling on the floor until the flames fall off. You should assist them with the roll at the ankles, not the waist area.

The lesson should end with a wrap up on the skills learned and each child should get either a shirt sticker or certificate of completion. A generous budget or sponsor can even make some fire safety activity books available. This keeps a positive ending to the event and will trigger some discussion and reinforcement when they return home.

Ages 5–12: Elementary School Level

This is another important element of your public education program. Time is still available to be part of the scheduled learning periods and students are at their peak absorption rates for your lessons.

Identify all the locations within your district, be they public, parochial, private, charter, or home- schooled sites. The best way to get accepted into the school is to have an outline and other elements of your program available for review by the school's curriculum director. We had one faith-based school that disqualified a video with a funny Dracula, as it was contrary to their teachings. They will approve the format and make suggestions to meet the time restraints and scheduling.

You must adhere to their time limits if you expect to be invited back. An assembly type presentation is most likely to be the format you need to follow when educating several hundred students at one location. Check the room ahead of time and be sure you can work the lights and audio/visual equipment or have one of the school's IT people present to help.

You should get an introduction by the principal or program director, so have a brief bio with your name for their use. A lecture type format is good to start off with and try to support it with a PowerPoint or slide presentation. Focus on a few home fire safety points and have at least a three-year cycle of presentations in your bag of tricks. You may be seeing these students several times over the next few years, so you want fresh and new material to keep their attention.

An investment in some good quality videos will be needed, as these should be part of your reinforcement of the message quadrant. Videos can be purchased from Nation Fire Protection Association (NFPA) and free or low-cost ones can be found on various government fire websites and from insurance companies. You may also want to pool resources with neighboring fire agencies and other regional fire groups to spread out the costs and ensure a variety of films.

The topics should include: fire prevention, escape planning, smoke alarms, home alone practices, calling 9-1-1, careless smoking, fire play, cooking, electrical appliance safety, crawling low under smoke, stop, drop, and roll, vehicle safety, campfires, power equipment safety, and other points that you will find in the curriculum and through experiences on the job.

Each year's Fire Prevention Week will highlight a topic that should be supported in your talks and with banners, press releases, and handouts throughout your district. These group presentations may be intimidating at first, but you will get better each time as your public speaking skills are refined.

Fire drills should also be overseen at least once a year at the schools, timed and evaluated. You can even have some cardboard flames made up to block an exit area so the teachers and students will be challenged to find another way out. The attendance or head count procedures can also be spiced up a bit by taking one of the older students out of line as they are exiting the building. Be sure the principal or fire safety coordinator is aware of this and stay in plain sight with the student until the responsible teacher does their count.

Ages 12–18: Middle School and High Schools

These age levels are the most difficult to get scheduled and are not for the faint of heart or new instructor. The schedules are pretty filled up with demands for teaching, labs, lunches, and testing, so it may be hard to get a time slot. Many times the schools will have a professional company come in that is paid for by the school district or supporting agency. You should try and be included to endorse the event and observe the methodology used to reach this target group.

When the fire tragedy occurred at Seton Hall University's Boland Hall in 2000 resulting in the death of three students and fifty injuries, four of which were serious, we saw a need to develop a Dorm Fire Safety Program for college bound seniors, and we were welcomed to present the program every year to the senior class. The program was run at the beginning of the school day and included two presenters, easel charts, video, and brochures. Dorm fire safety education should be a priority nationwide, as dorms can be a wild place with lots of parties, alcohol use, intruders, and poor decision making being rampant. New Jersey Division of Fire Safety adopted a fire sprinkler retrofit regulation for college residential housing and requirements for emergency planning and fire resistive furniture. Many states and learning institutions have not adopted these life safety regulations, and we will continue to see more tragedies during what should be the highlights of a person's educational pursuits. Off campus housing and frat houses will not be regulated much, if at all, and fires in these smaller, older buildings will continue to take lives and cause injuries.

You can make a difference by educating the students about escape planning, building safety features, fire drills, safe parties, smoke alarms, proper disposal of smoking materials, taking out the trash, candles, incense, and extension cords.

A presentation or flyer to parents would also be helpful to get the message out about selecting fire safe dorms. You could also encourage them to include a combination smoke and carbon monoxide alarm with a sealed battery, flashlight, whistle, and duct tape in their college care package. There are several packaged programs available through United States Fire Administration (USFA), NFPA, and fire marshals that include everything you will need to gain quick approvals from your educational administrators.

Education Programs for Adults Including Senior Citizens

Fire safety presentations can continue for adults if you have a good speaker's bureau and make yourself available evenings and weekends. Various clubs and fraternal organizations often have an educational portion of their regular meetings that can be hard to fill. Here is your opportunity to promote the fire service, get a fire safety message out to the public, and maybe score a free dinner. Short and precise is the order of the day, discussing a recent fire that occurred locally or a fire that had a lot of media coverage. Adult schools may be another venue that can be one night or a series of presentations. Every event should have a brochure to take home that reinforces the lessons taught.

Senior citizens are another high-risk group that should always be included in your target audience. Fire deaths and burn injuries occur due to medications, slow reflexes, mental slowness, handicaps, thin skin, bad information, and carelessness are some of the reasons that bad events are second only to young children in occurrences. Many senior clubs and senior residential buildings have speakers in regularly and the group can be a lot of fun to interact with. An offering of cookies, cakes, or donuts always seems to swell the crowd, so check with the group's contact person to arrange refreshments.

Speak slow and clear so people with hearing loss or diminished capacities can follow your presentation and include a video made for that audience. We had a great video made with beloved comedian Jonathan Winters that was perfect for the senior groups. Many videos that are available include well-known personalities that add to the impact and reception of the message. The seniors have many stories, just like the preschoolers, so you may get off track with your message. Have an outline or easel chart to keep you on course. You can also enlist an aid or "plant" in the group who can ask a question about a point you may have missed.

Offering free home inspections and smoke alarms can be another way to get into those one family homes where most fire deaths and injuries occur. Entering these homes can be an experience. You may find super clean or super dirty conditions, hoarding, pets, non-ambulatory residents, stair lifts, stuck windows, no smoke alarms, and no railings among other things that can set your mind reeling when it comes to safety.

Throw rugs are very common items that cause falls with seniors, and one time I met a retired World War II marine veteran at his home to inspect his furnace. He opened the complicated door configuration, and as I opened the storm door, he was moving backward from the main door and got entangled with a throw rug. He was out of reach, and I could not react fast enough to grab him, and he fell to the floor breaking a hip. He had some great stories and salty language while we waited for EMS to arrive. I thought to myself here is a guy who survived numerous battles unscathed and then gets injured in his own home from a nasty throw rug. So be prepared for almost anything when doing the senior circuit, but also take time to enjoy their life experiences and fascinating war stories.

Educating the Public via Media Outreach in Fire Houses

Having a public information officer (PIO) is essential for every organization. This person will have training in the what, where, when, who, and why that the press demands for all stories.

Your prepared releases are a story about ways to prevent fires, avoid burns, make your home safer, cook safely, and escape a burning building. You can have a series of seasonal releases, annual reports, current fire trends, but have many. A year's worth of articles to rotate with some refreshing or ties to local incidents is the bare minimum that should be part of a complete public outreach program. The introduction of high power batteries in vehicles, telephones, toys, and tools, along with other new technologies are a rapidly evolving area of education.

Pictures with proper captions and names will go a long way to getting the articles published and get the reader's attention. The more people in the picture the better, it sells papers.

Take your local editor to lunch and establish contacts with all the reporters and photographers. You need to know what format is the best for print and picture processing by the publishers. Digital or electronic transmission of your material is the most required way to be submitted, as it makes the layout staff's job easier and quicker. The old days of dropping off an article with 35mm pictures or faxing articles are long gone. Be sure the articles are accurate, professional, proofread, and contain contact information. The articles should also include a quote from your boss to speed the approval process along.

Other places to get the message out include: homeowner's association newsletters, school newspaper, local cable TV, department website, social media accounts, envelope stuffers in government mailings, literature racks in public buildings, banners, window posters, and school poster contests. Maybe if you are good and get lucky, you may even get your own column.

Breaking news calls to your contacts must follow department guidelines, lest you run afoul of the chief or other superior who wants the glory. There is no such thing as "off the record." If you say it, then it can appear anywhere and often not in the context you wanted. Speak slowly and deliberately using easily understood words without too many technical terms. Today's fast-paced social media can lead to hard to retract statements and pictures, so be ready at all times or say "I'll have to get back to you" and then be sure you do.

The transparency rules such as Open Public Records Act (OPRA) also mean that pretty much everything you e-mail, file, print, photograph, document, or sneeze on is open to public scrutiny, so honesty is always the best policy. There are times when you will not know the answer or an investigation is underway and the official statement must wait.

The *Grande* Events

The last area of public education is the open houses or safety fair concept. These will be big undertakings that require a lot of coordination and help from many sources. They can occur at your fire headquarters, schools, parking lots, recreation centers, or other large venue locations. Look for bathrooms, table space, parking/mass transit access, indoor demonstration areas, electrical power, dressing rooms, kitchen and water supply, garbage cans, a sitting area with tent, and high visibility as key components for the ideal site.

The open house events can include various safety organizations that can display their equipment and hand out literature, including police, EMS, Forest Fire Service (Smokey Bear), Red Cross, Hospitals, Burn Center, Fire Sprinkler Trailers, Smoke House Trailers, and Shriners to name just a few that will gladly participate.

Contact your local insurance companies that have outreach programs and safety supplies to hand out. Local Chamber of Commerce will have merchants that can help with goodie bags, refreshments, fun stuff for kids, costume characters, raffles, publicity, and many other crowd attractors. Your local child level gym may provide mats and instructors for stop, drop, and roll and crawling low under smoke practice.

The event should be a Friday night or Saturday afternoon so school work and family obligations will not be impacted, but whatever day and time you can schedule will work out. You may want to tie this in with Fire Prevention Week. Check on competing events in the immediate neighborhood so you have good access and cooperation from all who live or work in the area.

For emergency apparatus displays, be sure egress routes are planned for the vehicles unless they are dedicated to the event for the duration. Vehicles should have personnel assigned to them at all times to prevent damage and the constant sound of air horns and sirens. Be sure wheels are chocked and drug lockers and portable radios are secured.

Some other things to plan for are traffic control, exterior lighting, portable sound system, photographers, and an old stove as a prop for showing how to extinguish a grease fire. You can do a ladder rescue from a second floor window, squirt water at a "flame" target, and do fire gear demonstrations. Have plenty of staffing to answer questions, run demonstrations, and help with set up and clean up. A small area separate from the main floor could be set up to show video or give short demonstrations and lectures.

A face painting station is always a big hit and this can be done through a local salon or other con- tact that you may find. A live Dalmatian dog for pictures can also be a big hit and a chance to provide historical information on these dogs.

Post a schedule of events with times and locations for all the various stations. All the vendors should be given publicity the night of the event via signs and handouts. The following week should include personal thank-you letters and articles with pictures in the newspapers, on websites, and social media. This will be a high energy, informative, and well-received affair that will become a tradition.

Another type of event is the safety expo, and this can have many versions. We did a Transportation Expo one year in a parking lot beside a railroad siding. Conrail brought a locomotive with a box car movie theater followed by a caboose. The children got to see and climb on a real train and then watch a train track safety video in the box car. NJ Transit brought a commuter bus to show kids how to act on a bus and the many safety features of modern mass transit. Many of these kids had never been in a bus before!

We of course had fire trucks, EMS/rescue vehicles, DPW trucks, and police doing bicycle safety. Burger King even supplied us with food for the day. There were children from a summer recreation pro- gram, local day cares, and walk-ins that enjoyed and learned a lot about transportation safety and we had fun too.

At another event NJ Transit sent Cool Cat, a retired Radio City Rockette, who really connected with the kids and did a rail safety skit on stage with a simulated car approaching a train crossing and making the right decisions. She was a big hit with the kids and the firefighters. I still have my autographed poster on the wall. These resources are usually available from whatever transportation group services your area. Just be sure and ask far enough ahead to help scheduling.

Juvenile Fire Setter Intervention Program

This is a very special group of individuals that require a seasoned educator who can connect with the students and induce behavioral changes. Most of the attendees are mandated by a local law enforcement agreement due to a fire-related or malicious mischief offense. The ages will be from about ten years old to eighteen, mostly males, possible learning disabilities, disrupted family environments, group followers, or mentally unbalanced.

Many national courses adopted by fire departments have a mental health evaluation portion to identify the level of risk to their families and the community. This should be left to trained professionals who are licensed to spot severe emotional problems and possible psychotic behaviors. Most of the referrals you get will be the result of curiosity fire play or poor group decision making. Parents and juvenile justice agencies want to implement intervention programs that correct bad behavior while avoiding courts and fines. This is especially true for first time offenders and parental requests for a child they caught playing with matches.

These courses are best taught with two instructors, and class size should be limited to twelve. You may want to team up with neighboring towns for instructors, videos, classrooms, and other resources. This interagency coordination can help get students into a class sooner so that the effect of their transgressions is more immediately felt. A private classroom with media equipment is the best way to exhibit professionalism and gain the student's focus. Name placards, paper and pencils, course outline, and water should be placed for each student.

A guest or keynote speaker could also really up the impact of your message. Look for someone who was injured by fire, had a relative impacted by fire, or a burn educator. We had a local corporate lawyer and library president who was involved in a laboratory accident while in college. He lost both hands, almost died, and has lived with prostheses for over sixty years. His presentation was awesome, reliving his nightmare and providing an inspirational story of survival and forgiveness. Thanks, Anthony!

You will find this a challenging group to engage, so brush up on your teaching skills for special needs students including ADHD, Asperger's syndrome, and other learning impediments that you should identify ahead of time. The Juvenile Fire Setter Intervention Course outline I have included at the end of this chapter, was created after attending instructor training and doing actual courses. The contact time should be about three hours and include homework. This course is educational and punitive in nature.

I have also included the "About Me Activity" worksheet, which is designed to be an icebreaker and give you some insight into the group's mindset. This activity should be done anonymously and collected to be read in front of the class. This sheet can also be used in team-building scenarios and other group activities. Be ready for some questions on the questions. Remember this group is not usually your honor students and vocabulary skills may be limited.

Videos should be used to reinforce the message and give their brains a rest from the instructor. We also used news footage at times and found many sources for current fires that included injuries and fatalities. You are trying to drive home a point, so don't be bashful about shocking the audience.

The homework or essay part is important for you and the students. You need feedback on what is being learned and understood. The students need to reinforce their lessons and let you know they will improve their behaviors. A wise teacher informed me to be sure and specify typed format along with spacing, font size, and length; otherwise you will get three pages with large letters and three or four sentences per page. You should also watch for copy-and-paste essays that are plagiarized from the Internet.

A Juvenile Fire Setter Intervention program may be the hardest to implement, but the returns are unlimited. You may just correct a behavior that could kill or injure an entire family. You may be putting a person back on the right track for life and you could make a friend forever. You may influence that person to further their education and look at the fire service in a whole new light.

Special Event Invitations

There will be events sponsored by other organizations and can include health, science and history fairs, open houses, PTO meetings, and big truck expos. Look for these events to be involved with both for support activities and as an actual presenter.

These could include speaking, display table, video, fire trucks, and being the "Fire Answer Man."

Student government day is when the local high school class officers take over local government for the day as mayor, fire chief, purchasing agent, and other positions that keep a town or city operating. This is a fun day and a chance to work with future leaders. You will have several hours to speak with them and promote your department. Do not miss this opportunity to be with intelligent and personable students who may one day be a co-worker or even your boss! They will speak to their family, friends, teachers, and the sponsors of the event so your presentation should be professional and thorough.

These programs give you more chances to put your best foot forward and instill admiration and confidence for what you and your department does every day to make your little section of the world a better place.

Keep a scrapbook of these efforts. These articles can be used for grant and funding requests and for awards documentation. Memory books can also be used to rev up your energy level and be shared with family members and friends who want to know more about your career. Your legacy is important. Leave a trail for others to follow. There are fifty-two weeks in the year that are available for outreach. Fire never takes a holiday!

11

Juvenile Fire Setter Intervention Course Outline

I. **Introduction of instructors**

    A. Job description and duties
    B. Certifications to instruct

II. **Why are you here?**

    A. Agreement with parents and prosecutor
    B. Alternatives to program
    C. Social ramifications of actions
        1. Family life
        2. Friends
        3. Employment now and future
    D. What should you get out of this course?
        1. "About Me Activity" (anonymous)
        2. Alternatives for leisure time and hanging out
        3. Counseling and mental health agencies referrals
        4. Your future as a good citizen
        5. Surviving adolescence and peer pressure

Show short, shock-type, fire safety video with injuries or fatalities.
Guest speaker: Someone who was injured by fire or treats burn victims.

I. **What is fire?**

    A. Fire triangle and fire tetrahedron (easel chart or white board)
    B. Good fire vs. bad fire
    C. Why fire excites
    D. Fires in history
        1. Warfare
        2. Rome and other big city fires like Chicago
        3. Fires in the United States annual rates and types (easel chart or white board)
        4. How and why fire departments were formed: The future of fire suppression

Video: fire department history and/or fire suppression content
Break for ten to fifteen minutes

V. **Fire prevention**

    A. Candle safety
    B. Smoking
    C. Flammable liquids
    D. Campfires and BBQs
    E. Fireplaces and chimneys
    F. Lighters and matches
    G. Fireworks
    H. Storage of combustibles
    I. Criminals and arson
    J. Show video fire safety topics, safe practices and this could be presented in a cartoon style, to lighten the subject matter

V. **Review of topics**

    A. Questions and answers

B. Assignment of essay
   1. Three pages' double spaced maximum font of 14
   2. Use above outline for content
   3. Due back to instructors ________________
   4. Parent or guardian should sign bottom of essay

12

About Me Worksheet

Q: Where would you like to be right now?

____

____

Q: What do you want to happen in your life?

____

____

Q: If you could accomplish anything, what would it be?

____

____

Q: If you could change your first name, what would it be

____

____

Q: If you could be invisible for one hour, what would you do?

____

____

Q: What do you like to do when you are alone?

____

____

Q: What makes you feel good?

____

____

Q: Are your ancestors proud of you?

____

____

Q: If you could take a time machine anywhere, where would you go?

____

____

Q: What age would you like to be right now?

____

____

Q: What makes you laugh?

____

____

Q: What makes you cry?

____

____

Q: What three things do you like about yourself?

____

____

Q: If you could go anywhere, all expenses paid, where would you go?

____

____

Acknowledgments and Final Thoughts

Many people helped me with encouragement, technical advice, proofreading, editing, and support. First, I want to thank my wife, Dianne, for her countless hours of editing and ongoing input into this project. Without her thirty-five years of support, this book would not exist.

Big thanks to my parents, brother, educators, instructors, authors, mentors, and friends who helped to educate me and shape my work ethic and opinions. Anthony Buccino for sharing all his editing and literary experience. John Simko for showing me how to say more with less. Joey Bee for his support, friendship, and technical editing. Carole Brown and Patrick Potter for editing and technical advice on animals. Susan and Jack Farr for technical animal advice and encouragement. Glenn Darden for his input and eye-opening discussions. My co-workers in Fire, EMS, Code Enforcement and Police, it was an honor to work with you all. Commissioner/Senator Carmen A. Orechio for the opportunity to serve.

Mary Ann Shepard-Romas for her input and preserving the "fire family" scrapbook from Captain John Frobose. This 1940s era collection of newspaper articles and pictures when compared to my scrap-book fifty years later, supports the phrase: "The more things change, the more they stay the same." We still need to shovel out fire hydrants, be careful with candles, cook safely, practice fire drills, dispose of ashes and tobacco safely, read the warning labels on containers, install and test smoke alarms, lobby for better building construction and fire sprinklers, install and test carbon monoxide alarms, pull to the side of the road for responding emergency vehicles, review owner's manual for equipment, make your home childproof, teach your children about fire safety, and follow fire prevention rules throughout the years.

"The late Fire Chief Alan Brunacini was an advocate for fire prevention. He felt that no one would be hurt by those fires that never occurred. Resources and effort put into fire prevention programs have paid dividends that can never be measured. However, when you review the fire death and injury statistics over the past several decades, you can see a downward trend, which many like Chief Brunacini attributed to efforts in the area of fire prevention.

Let me urge you to support the fire prevention efforts in your community."
Dr Harry Carter Firehouse 11/1/2017

About the Author
Lt. David A Wilson

Inspired by family, friends, and Emerson's poem "Success," David Wilson, a lifelong Nutley resident (LLNR), began his service career in 1974 joining the Nutley Volunteer Emergency & Rescue Squad, becoming an EMT, treasurer, crew chief, training officer, day captain, serving on many committees, and meeting his wife, Dianne. The American Red Cross provided more opportunities to serve, donating blood, volunteering on the Board of Directors, and becoming chairman of building and grounds. David also served as deacon at Franklin Reformed Church.

In 1980, he began working at H&R Block as a tax preparer, instructor, public information coordinator, office supervisor, and specialist in IRS audits. He was appointed by the Nutley Board of Education as Treasurer of School Monies for twenty-seven years, beginning in 1986. He prepared monthly audits and financial reports for the district.

In 1985, Commissioner Carmen A. Orechio appointed David as Nutley Fire Department fire inspector. Here was a career where his mechanical background from Lincoln Technical Institute, public speaking, financial training, love of people, and the need to make the world a better and safer place all came together. He was certified as a fire official, arson investigator, instructor, Haz Mat technician, fire sub code official, housing official, along with being the deputy coordinator with OEM. His many fire investigations led David to create a Burn Avoidance educational program for all preschoolers, a Dorm Fire Safety program for college-bound seniors, Juvenile Fire Setter Intervention program, and Senior Citizen Fire Safety. He wrote monthly safety and preparedness articles for local papers, radio, and cable shows. Functioning as the damage assessment coordinator, he arranged over two million dollars in FEMA and insurance grants that reimbursed Nutley for disaster losses. In 2007, he was promoted to lieutenant, retiring in 2010. He worked through 2016 as fire sub code official for Nutley Code Enforcement overseeing permits for new and renovated properties and field inspecting for compliance. "So You Want to Be a Fire Inspector?" written by David and published by *Fire Engineering Magazine* in 2009. He also had articles in *Firehouse*, *Time*, and *Nutley Neighbors Magazine*.

He appears on JOEYBEE.TV as Organic Gardening with Inspector Dave, teaching healthy, low-cost, and time-friendly backyard gardening and bird feeding. A passion for local history research has led to an alliance with Town Historian John Demmer. Together, they do local history walks, lectures at the library, preserve Nutley artifacts, and appear on YouTube. Dave served on the Municipal Tree Inventory Committee.

David was awarded by Nutley Jaycees, Nutley Rotary, Knights of Columbus, NJ Citizens Alliance for Fire Safety, Nutley Elks, American Legion, VFW, American Red Cross, Nutley Emergency and Rescue Squad, H&R Block, Nutley Board of Commissioners, and New Jersey State Legislature.